THE UNBEARABLE UNLIKENESS OF BEING

A DEVIANT GUIDE TO MARRIAGE

JEAN WOLF

The Unbearable Unlikeness of Being: A Deviant Guide to Marriage
© 2003, Jean Wolf. All rights reserved.
Published by SassyGirl Press, St. Paul, Minnesota

ISBN 978-0-578-72744-8 (paperback)
Library of Congress Control Number: 2020914109

Cover art by Jean Wolf.

CONTENTS

PREFACE

Marriage today is a twister. It entwines, deviates, knots, bends, contorts, curves, coils and changes shapes. It's full of crooks and kinks. It swerves, then reverses. You may believe that it's one thing; then it turns out to be another. Yet everyone seems to think they understand it because like the weather, marriage is ubiquitous. People worry about it, talk about it and hang around in it, but that doesn't mean they know a thing. El Niño this, cold front that. The meteorologists who may actually comprehend these phenomena make accurate long-term predictions about as frequently as snow falls in Key West.

And that's about the same success rate that we marriage counselors have in predicting the outcome of a marriage. The intimates of the couple do no better in their predictions, and the wedding itself is just a distraction. When the day comes, so do the guests, cousins and friends, who often use the occasion to find mating prospects for themselves. They wish the couple everlasting joy and fulfillment, the absence of which can go largely undetected for years, not only by the wedding guests who are not paying attention anymore because they are caught up in their own problems and quests, but by the couple themselves who may be floating in a shallow pond of indifference or in deeper waters of despair. The couple avoids taking a keen look at their condition, possibly because conflict is unsavory or because they are busy at the gym.

Still others may be busy with babies and toddlers. In spite of the low birth rate, the occasional couple still marries to have children. The purpose of marriage was clear-cut when the majority of people married to breed. They just tumbled into their rabbit holes and emerged with a litter. Not anymore. Now such behavior is considered ecologically unsound or déclassé. This often leaves the couple without anchor or compass in their marriages, hence floundering for purpose. We don't know what they are doing in that rabbit hole; we know little about their mating habits. In fact, we know more about the mating habits of Tasmanian frogs than we do of our married neighbors.

We also do not know whether our neighbors' marriage is democratic. Totalitarian rule is simpler because it efficiently handles the mess of second opinions. A few marriages may still be totalitarian. We cannot be sure. With such scant information about what their friends, relatives and neighbors are doing on the political and libidinal fronts, some people resort to reading about celebrity marriages in the *National Enquirer*. (Although few admit to this, it is the reason for all of those extraneous trips to the grocery store.) As engaging as this activity may be, it has proven to provide insufficient guidance for the average couple.

Frankly, it's about time someone straightened this out: What's with marriage today? In a nearly heroic effort, our team at the Forum for the Advancement of Better Relationships Through Testing, Counseling and Research has been struggling with these issues. A few years ago, we launched a study to explore the prickly and unwieldy aspects of coupling that we have encountered in our practice and to translate our findings into a useful guide for you. Today the shelves of bookstores and libraries are filled with books about marriage and love, but the work of other marriage specialists lacks the grit and common sense of our team's work. We believe that we have developed a keen grasp of the issues facing the modern couple and trust that the reader will benefit from our innovative research and rich insight.

One final note: In writing this guide to marriage, not only have I my crafty and resourceful associates to thank, but also my husband Jake, a patient man, who seems remarkably unconcerned that during this protracted endeavor, I have been spinning in my own orbit.

Prudence E. Nestleweiss
Forum for the Advancement of Better Relationships
Through Counseling, Testing and Research
St. Paul, Minnesota

Introduction

THE MYSTERIES OF THE MARRIED

As my associates and I studied the phenomenon of marriage and its prospects for the future, we found the institution in a fragile state and its practical aspects disheartening. Like the assorted couples who consult us, you too may be flummoxed by the thorny patches in your relationship. With that in mind, our team has spent the last few years exploring marriage and developing this uncommon guide for couples using every means we could concoct—questionnaires, case studies, field research, anything short of espionage (well, even a little of that). You need all the help you can get to manage in the socially contrived, jerry-built institution of marriage. For centuries it has been precariously balanced upon the expectation that two persons mate for life, an expectation which invites disappointment and defies common sense.

At the Forum for the Advancement of Better Relationships Through Counseling, Testing and Research, better known as FABRCTR, our team members are Rose Ellen Bloom, H. Daniel

Doppelmann, Victoria Regis-Rittenhouse, Howie Sack and me, Pru Nestleweiss.[1] Here's how we hatched: Fifteen years ago after Sack and I had worked together for a few years at a marital counseling center run by Otto the Autocrat, we cast an escape plan. When we told Bloom and Doppelmann about it—they had only recently been hired and we noted that they were looking more haggard by the day—they were cheered by the plan and signed on. So while Otto was engaged in devising ever more draconian rules about dress code, posture and bathroom breaks for his staff, we looked for office space and eventually settled in a deserted church. Previously it had sufficed not only as a home for the Presbyterians, but as a lair for Jesse James and his minions in the twenties, and later a Jewish mortuary, a small experimental community theater, a ballet studio and a homeless shelter, in that order. We found it in a hapless state, but considered it rife with possibility. Well, Doppelmann did. He knew from his first glance that the choir loft, still more or less intact, would serve as a retreat from our beleaguered couples and a worthy spot for case consultation.

After the renovation was completed, we hired Eddie, a young, homeless man who had lingered on and pestered us, to be our receptionist. We would find him curled up in the shrubbery or on Sack's couch, his scavenged food in our refrigerator and his bedroll under my desk. Defeated repeatedly in our efforts to evict him, we changed course. He served

---

[1] To be perfectly candid, one of our team members originally objected to our clinic's acronym. Bloom believed that the public and especially our readers, might think that we're simply fabricating tales when we're actually doing serious research. Sack said she had a point. The rest of us couldn't get too worked up about it. "Fabricated tales are better than real ones anyway," said Doppelmann.

us reasonably well for a year or so, then drifted off. Now we are ably served by Holly Hollingsworth.

Let me introduce you to our team members:

Bloom, 48, is a somewhat fleshy, hard-working woman whose oversized glasses tend to inch down the slope of her nose. Somewhat anxious, she prefers order to disorder and has a habit of straightening framed diplomas, especially her own. While she doesn't happen to like body piercing, nude beaches or red meat, she respects the rights of others to partake. The team is grateful to her for her conscientious and charitable nature. She is married to Al who visits the church periodically to check on her. They have two fair-haired teenage daughters about to burst into their own.

Doppelmann, 45, is a tall, slender man. He is not exactly attractive, although given his variable nature, he has moments of princely appeal. He can be—and frequently is—seized by his imagination and by the beauty, mystery and majesty of the spheres. To be candid, he suffers from an incontinent psyche, but he cannot help it. This condition can be serious and require some management by the rest of our team, but up to this point we have not deemed medication necessary. He is in his second marriage, this to Nedra, whom he refers to as his *rara avis.* Just one look at her and you know she is a psychic in one of those basement hovels where ropes of beads curtain the doorways, but you will be wrong. She is a bookkeeper at Copy Tech.

Regis-Rittenhouse, our arriviste, is a woman of uncertain age. Lean and handsome, she is as tall as Doppelmann. Unlike Doppelmann, she is rarely seized by her imagination, but she can be seized by other things, things like her colleagues' faulty logic. After twenty years in the Air Force as an information specialist, she attended graduate school and joined our staff just three years ago. We appreciate her acute intellect, and we are acclimating to her withering, deadpan remarks. Although she has yet to admit it, she has at least three cats.

Sack, 59, is a slightly balding, cherubic-appearing man who slumps when he is depressed. After he and his wife Shirley separated, a few months before we began our research, he was slumping quite frequently and, to Bloom's dismay, smoking again. Apparently his wife grew weary of his gloomy, rather dependent nature, so after sharing 27 years, three children and a menagerie of pets with him, she is gone, leaving Sack with his aging basset hound, Hobbes, the last of the menagerie. Still, we remind him, it is just a separation and hope remains.

I am the final member of the team and its scribe, that is, the person who has transcribed, edited and interpreted our work for you. Although it once seemed certain that Regis-Rittenhouse would command this position, she deferred because, she said, she had to put all of her energy into preventing our team from stumbling over its own excesses. As it became increasingly clear that my partners expected me to pinch hit, I agreed, but with the stipulation that I can render matters as I see them. They have generously given me a free hand in reporting our discussions, case studies and research with the sole request that their insights and invention be duly noted. I am long married to Jake. In spite of a few unorthodox habits, we seem to have found equilibrium often enough to survive as a couple, but not so often that conjugal stupor sets in.

Finally, there is the sylphine Holly. Doppelmann was performing in a community theater production of the musical *Nunsense* about the time Eddie drifted off. He had always wanted to dress up like a nun and because he has quite a nice falsetto voice, he was selected for a part. Holly, 23, played one of the younger nuns. Unable to pay rent out of income from an occasional radio-advertizing gig, she was grateful when Doppelmann offered her the job. Not only has she adapted admirably to the team, but she can distract squabbling couples in the waiting room with a few bars from *Camelot*.

Down to Business

Now that you have met our able team, it is time to explain our work. After we escaped Otto's grip and set up our practice, we increasingly noticed that the state of marriage counseling and research isn't all it could be. First of all, problems that pop up as randomly but predictably as dandelions on your lawn—problems like mind reading, naps and quirks—are sadly neglected by our colleagues in the field. And not one of them has ever grappled publicly with the universal issues of hearing acuity, memory half-life and audible crunching. Instead, they trot out unrealistic expectations such as these: It is possible for your partner to heed your sensible advice, to understand what you mean, to even *want* to understand what you mean or to buy the right brand of toothpaste.

Our colleagues, however, are not completely to blame for unrealistic expectations. The demographers have a role in this; they tell us that about half of marriages actually last. Given the diverse and abundant opportunities for them to fail, our team finds this alleged success rate suspiciously high, which leads us to question both the veracity and the competence of the demographers. As if these implausible statistics of the already married were not enough of a problem, growing numbers of young adults—our future leaders—are not even marrying in the first place. And the theft of wives, once a reassuring example of the popularity of marriage, is no longer widespread.

Marriage not only suffers from waning enthusiasm, but from a poor premise. This leads us to a second complaint about our colleagues. They have turned a blind eye to the precarious underpinning of marriage: monogamy. In the animal world we find insignificant support for this as a natural state. Humans in nearly every culture have doggedly persisted in the ritual of marriage, a union in which monogamy is often expected from at least one of the partners, in spite of our similarity to the chimpanzees who are reputedly unfaithful mates. Cats, unlike humans, make no pretense whatsoever of mating for life. The average female cat has a brief tryst with any tomcat that happens along, then bears and feeds their mutual offspring without giving the father a whisker of a thought. Meanwhile, the tom continues to loiter, chase and fornicate in assorted neighborhoods until he is annihilated by other tomcats or until his human owners cart him off to the local veterinarian for invasive surgery.

The black vulture, on the other hand, does mate for life. Thirty-five million households in this country have at least one cat and only a trifling number have a black vulture. We could use these statistics to inform ourselves, but no one seems to be paying much attention. Hypocrisy and denial may be operating or perhaps human affection for cats is some form of wish fulfillment.

Our third complaint concerns the sorry definitions of marriage in current use. When we settled into the loft for our first discussion, we immediately discarded the moldy, outdated definitions that inhabit the literature and formulated our own, one more fluid and reflective of the times:

> **Marriage** *is a union commonly composed of two people, and if so, one from each gender, but not always; who probably live together and who plan to be together in the future, at least for the time being (see Glossary).*

Our original plan was to study normal marriages, but we could not find any. We began by looking at our own. Sack's is certainly in a state of confusion and instability, and everyone knows that neither Doppelmann nor I have a normal marriage. We were surprised when Bloom confessed that even her marriage is not particularly normal, but she probably just said that to fit in. And Regis-Rittenhouse, a hyphenate, carries around that cumbersome surname even though she is single. Our patients as a group are a little more normal than we are, but not significantly, so we settled for a study of normal neurotic pairs.

And that seems to include nearly everyone. We explored the marriages of coots, crones, crabs, hipsters, lobsters, mobsters, monsters, couples who seem like singles because one or both are hardly there, couples who seem like threesomes because one of them is always thinking about someone else, actual threesomes who think they are a couple, and couples who spin around each other like binary asteroids.

Mystery

Bear with me for one final complaint. Other scholars of marriage purport to have the means to figure out whether two people will get along together in the future. They assess the compatibility of a couple by using inventories such as the Quickie Couple Compatibility Questionnaire, the Renegade Relationship Inventory and the Three-and-a-Half Step Premarital Assessment. "Poseurs all of them," sniffs Doppelmann, "arid, uninventive, stuffy, paper-shuffling researchers. Their explorations suffer from myopia and anemia. Where is the broader, the deeper, the richer vision? We must look at the *mystery* of relationships." He is right; other researchers do avoid mystery, perhaps out of fear or arrogance. Of course, it is a little tricky to measure accurately; nevertheless, we have attended to the mystery of marriage throughout our comprehensive and groundbreaking exploration.

Doppelmann had a case apropos. Not long ago he treated Birdie and Glen, a recently married couple. During their first appointment, Glen cowered slightly as Birdie complained exhaustively about his personal habits, hobbies and general distractibility. After Doppelmann had observed her steady stream of niggling for several minutes, he asked Glen why he tolerated it. The young man looked at Birdie poignantly, mist in his eyes, and sighed, "She is so beautiful." Doppelmann looked at Birdie himself, squinted and strained to see it. What he saw was a rather pale, flat-faced woman with pinpoint eyes and disappearing lips. Isn't it wonderful, he thought, her husband thinks she's beautiful. And instantly images of El Greco's great masterpieces colonized Doppelmann's consciousness: El Greco, the seventeenth-century painter believed by some to have had a vision problem because the human figures in his work are elongated. "And yet what great art it is!" he exclaimed aloud. His outburst startled both Birdie and Glen, but it startled Doppelmann even more. He prefers to keep his mental meanderings hidden while he is working with couples, but in spite of the awkward moment, his exclamation apparently came across as some sort of compliment to Birdie. They all recovered quite nicely.

Distorted vision may help many couples stay together, and it is no doubt exactly what drew them together in the first place. The members of our team have respect for this mystery and all the other mysteries that seem to inhabit the hearts and minds of the married. While some marriage counselors are preoccupied with saving marriages, we consider it sometimes foolish to meddle because far more marriages succeed than logic warrants. If we are heedless of the mystery, tampering with a couple's patterns could be counterproductive. Take an average couple, the Littles. Traci is offended when her husband Hank leaves his shoes by the TV set in the living room. Her sensibilities are injured, seemingly beyond repair, and she loses her sexual desire, often for weeks. Hank is puzzled by this reaction, especially in light of the basket of laundry which she regularly deposits near his shoes. There it sits until the next episode of *Buffy the Vampire Slayer* when she will fold it. Yet the Littles carry on.

"We should just leave these people alone," says Regis-Rittenhouse.

Chapter I

THE UNBEARABLE UNLIKENESS OF BEING

The essence of coupling is its main problem: The two people who join to make a life together are two *different* people. After the initial merger, a gradual awakening occurs as evidence mounts that the *us* is actually a you and a me. Even two people who seem similar are not and no one notices the differences more than they do. Worse yet, fresh differences keep emerging year after year. While this problem is more complex for straight people than gay people, it is, nevertheless, confounding and frequently quite startling for all couples. They are alarmed to find a kaleidoscope of disparities from bowling aptitude to the discard of Q-tips. This was not always the case. In simpler times, people paired off earlier while still young and malleable; they did not have the choice of 156 breakfast cereals or 213 television channels, everyone in town attended the same church, shoes stayed on until bedtime, and Q-tips were suspect, hence rarely used or discarded. Reader, you may reproach us for romancing the past here and no doubt the pilgrims and prairie settlers had their own problems with differences, but it has gotten worse. "Much worse," said Sack.

The team is uncertain whether this is distinctly a human problem, but we think it is. For example, a cluster of cloned rats looks just like a cluster of regular rats. This would not be true for a group of humans unless they were wearing burkas. Even a brief glance at a lineup of chorus girls or a string of uniformed football players is enough to confirm notable and intriguing differences among the individuals. And later when they emerge in street clothes, the players and dancers are as eclectic as the residents of Madame Tussauds.

Appearances notwithstanding, a couple often begins a marriage believing that two shall be one. When it is discovered that this is not only false, but that it is patently false, existential angst may overcome the unsuspecting couple. A mourning period ensues in which one of them takes to devouring banana chips and retires at 8 PM while the other assumes a beached-whale mode in front of the TV set until Miss Cleo signs off. Or worse, the couple camouflages their mourning in nasty verbal barrage. Some mutual view of reality must be adopted for détente, but what will it be and whose will it be? At this point it is particularly unfortunate if either or both of them shout, "Mine."

Our group approached this issue with sensitivity and trepidation. Since it seemed apparent that we should start with some right-brained activity to overcome our fears, get inside the idea and stimulate our inventive juices, I suggested that we rent *Being John Malkovitch* and watch it together. Regis-Rittenhouse dismissed the idea as frivolous and a ploy to avoid the tedium of serious research, but she relented when

we insisted that a fine film such as this one is serious literature and promised that we would read the script as well. Even
Bloom liked the idea as long as we got together on Al's bowling
night. (He likes to have her around when he is at home.)

Sack invited us to his house for the viewing. (This worked
reasonably well except that Hobbes, an intrusive, drooling
hound, was annoying.) The movie provided a forceful back-
drop for our exploration. People actually paid, then lined up
in cramped quarters for hours just to be inside the skin of
another person. In this case, inside the skin of a famous person. After the movie Sack wondered if anyone would line up to
be him and decided that no one would. Bloom consoled him
and said that she knows at least two or three people who would
probably love to be Sack for awhile. "Still, it's no lineup," he
said, "and my wife isn't one of them, is she?"

After nursing Sack back to equilibrium, we realized that
the movie's fantasy had an impact on all of us. It underscored
the disturbing fact that in our actual lives we can never become
someone else for awhile, feel what they feel, sense what they
sense, know what they know. Each of us has only our own
experience of the world and none of us will ever access the
experience of a lover or partner.

"If I could access Shirley's thoughts, I would know why she
prefers single life over her life with Hobbes and me," said Sack.

"Get over it," said Regis-Rittenhouse.

"Separateness is the painful reality that each married person discovers," Sack continued.

Dopplemann unwittingly scotched this exchange: "One
day there will be chips that we can insert into the human
brain ... chips that will duplicate the experience of a partner."

"Doppelmann, that's daffy," said Regis-Rittenhouse. "Think of the consequences for the international espionage scene. And for couples it would be more hazardous than helpful. How would they keep secrets from one another? They would have to renounce affairs, curtail shopping binges and admit depleting the caramel corn."

We called it quits for movie night and held our follow-up session in the choir loft where we are less angst-ridden than in alternative locations. Although Holly has made attempts to vitalize the loft by placing plants there, they haven't fared well because the place is windowless. (Those Presbyterians must have sung in the dark.) Bloom comes in with a watering can now and again. That helps. But not much.

We began making progress when we agreed to break things down by simply examining one difference at a time. We are marriage counselors, after all, not philosophers. Sometimes we are forced to think small, so we proceeded with a list of the nuts, bolts and Post-it Notes, the nitty-gritty of everyday life. As inconsequential as you may find any one of the items on our list, know that some couple somewhere has stumbled and yes, fallen because of it. Bloom went to the whiteboard—which Eddie had installed—and recorded the differences as we recalled them from our most notable cases:

orange-peeling style

grocery-shopping style

out of style

hearing acuity

finger dexterity

The Unbearable Unlikeness of Being

bladder control

driving aptitude

volleyball aptitude

verbal aptitude

attitude

propensity for disorder

anxiety over disorder

disorder

startle response

slow response

no response

random thinking

linear thinking

thinking

orgasm too early

orgasm too late

organism

fast-muscle twitch

slow-muscle twitch

nose twitch

testosterone level

income level

The Unbearable Unlikeness of Being

level playing field

time orientation

space orientation

political orientation

list dependency

espousal dependency

chemical dependency

short-term memory

long-term memory

false memory

small-talk repertoire

small talk

fast talk

kinetic energy

sexual energy

sexual malaise

apparel finesse

apparel ineptitude

missing apparel

room temperature

body temperature

body fat

audible body emissions

audible sighs

audible crunching

Our endeavor was beginning to feel like a sorry attempt to excavate every earthworm from an 80-acre cornfield. And besides, Bloom began drooping and her hand was cramping up. The completion of an exhaustive list of potential differences between two partners, differences that frequently lead to contention, was impossible, so we settled with what we had.

The impact of these differences varies from couple to couple. A wide discrepancy in volleyball aptitude may be a serious disappointment for one couple, yet may fail to surface in fifty years of marriage for another. Perhaps that couple has no interest in volleyball or would rather play cribbage or solitaire. Differences in orange-peeling style occur infrequently as well, but when they do, have been known to play a pivotal role in one partner's ascendancy within the relationship. More significant in this regard, however, are differences in bladder control. On car trips the issue catapults to the surface often causing partners to compete ferociously with one another for the longest holding period, all the while denying that they are competing. One woman, who had formerly outdone her husband with some consistency, had been humiliated with poor showings during her three pregnancies. After all of their babies had been born, she gave up drinking liquids a full day or two before trips to regain her status, but by then the couple had a carful of children whose bladders required so much attention that they forgot about their own.

Apparel issues, of course, are replete with differences. Partners are always dressing and undressing one another—well, literally too—but I mean with advice about what to wear or definitely not to wear. One has the eye of Versace, the other, the eye of a mole. Less familiar is the missing-apparel difference which might more accurately be called the lost-apparel difference, although the partner with the missing apparel will often not admit that the apparel is actually lost. A mother, meticulous in her own habits, might expect her 12-year old to leave her jacket at the ballfield, but when her spouse leaves his sweater—a pricey one that she gave him as a birthday gift—at the karate studio, on the bus, or for that matter, at the ballfield and says, "I can't remember … it'll show up," she may threaten divorce.

Some of the most intensely bitter quarrels have surfaced as a result of audible crunching with some partners failing to recognize that inaudible crunching is not even crunching. When I pointed this out to one of my clients, she said, "Of course it is and that's the difference between us. I can crunch inaudibly and he cannot." (This case had a poor outcome.)

Our team decided that we could not address all of these differences. We needed to look in-depth at just one or two. Regis-Rittenhouse was poised for this moment: "I have the perfect focus for our study: food consumption. Show me one relationship that doesn't struggle with this and one scholar of relationships who is dealing with it. It's virgin territory."

But couple disparities in food habits along with all of their preferences and repulsions proved to be too broad a topic. Some partners eat nothing but cream cheese and bagels; others are committed to the protection of endangered vegetables, consider all vegetables endangered, thereby eat none, and still others eat so indiscriminately that they will lunch on puppy chow. One never goes a day without freshly ground pepper; another will righteously assert that she never eats freshly ground pepper. Take-out, eat in, dinner at five, dinner at ten, no breakfast, a light brunch, pea soup for lunch, no desserts this month, candy bars for snacks, crab legs from shacks, ketchup on ice cream, just a bad dream, peanut butter at midnight, peanut butter to sleep tight, no butter, only margarine, no margarine, only butter and only if it's imported from France, fat chance, deviled eggs, fried eggs, scrambled eggs, a pox on eggs.

"How can we ever understand another person's eating habits?"

"Food," said Sack. "Only money is more complicated."

Well yes, money, source of carnage and comfort. No one had even mentioned it in the context of differences. But before we could respond, Regis-Rittenhouse went off on a tangent. She had discovered an article that described the work of researchers who had measured the density of taste buds on the tongues of their human subjects, thereby identifying super-tasters who have the highest density, medium-tasters and non-tasters with the lowest. Our team agreed that the implications of this distinction in a couple are profound. A super-taster is likely to be morbidly sensitive about food and contemptuous of the medium taster who is unable to distinguish subtle flavors and especially of the non-taster who needs a mouth aflame with hot pepper to know that he is not eating warm, buttered noodles. Like an artless and unsophisticated rustic, he is likely to eat everything on his plate, regardless of its quality. Scenarios of the worst-case situation, the coupling of a super-taster with a non-taster, are disquieting. Conditions would be ripe for the first to be snobbish or chronically critical and the second to appear poorly bred, an embarrassment to them both.

The team concurred that tastebud variation in marriage may be an issue far more prevalent than the public realizes and that marriage counselors have been remiss in their failure to identify it. As a result we began to slip inquiries about food and beverages into discussions with our couples. Bloom actually served snacks to hers, Sack managed to get himself invited for dinner a few times without directly asking—this temporarily lifted his spirits, and Doppelmann began spying on his couples in restaurants. We upbraided Doppelmann about that and warned him that his behavior could be misconstrued as stalking and thus sully the impeccable reputation of FABRCTR.

Still no suitable case emerged. Bloom was especially eager to find one so she could tell the unsuspecting couple that neither of them had to be inferior merely because their tasting characteristics differed. "After all, tongues are used for a lot of things besides tasting," she said, then blushed. Of course, we did not pursue the personal meaning of this comment for Bloom, but she had a salient point. A tongue is useful, if not actually essential, for a wide variety of activities and is sorely missed by any individual who loses one. Our discussion briefly went off track here as we tried to outdo one another in identifying the assorted uses of the human tongue.

But still, no case. Regis-Rittenhouse lost interest, and Doppelmann had disengaged after we censured his voyeurism.

"Only money is more complicated," Sack repeated, then left for a smoke.

We had been overlooking Sack again. And he was right. Snagged into the tongue discussion, we had been ignoring a pervasive difference problem. How could we have come this far in discussing couple differences without mentioning wealth, poverty, debt, budgets, bankruptcy, spenders, shoppers, misers and the lottery? Some couples share all of their money; others squirrel it away in arcane funds or secret little accounts. One partner plans for the future; another spends today. One tracks spending down to parking meter change; another remains resolutely oblivious to the source of money as well as its disposal. One is tight, another generous.

None of our cases seemed quite right for our flagship study on money differences until I realized that I had been sitting on it—the Case of the Hulking Barn. (Myopia, dear reader, sets in when the marriage counselor's case is too close to home.) After I told my team about it, the following was a go.

Lars and Kenya

Married for 25 years, Kenya, 48, and Lars, 54, have three teenage children. Kenya, a woman with an air of efficiency and purpose, is a manager in an advertising firm. She has been the primary breadwinner for many years. Lars is a winsome, aw-shucks kind of a guy, a throwback really. As for employment, he is pretty much resting on his laurels, but he doesn't see it that way. These laurels comprise six acres of property along with its house and barn—a barn of mythically large proportions—that he inherited in his early twenties from his grandfather. (The rest of the acreage somehow slipped out of family hands long ago. Lars never knew quite why, but there had been some talk of gambling debt.) He has puttered on the somewhat dilapidated, but ample 1880s farmhouse for years with the idea of restoring it to its original grandeur, which is difficult to do because it never was particularly grand. Nevertheless, he and Kenya have been raising three children there, and it suffices.

Lars works as an auctioneer from time to time, but his own needs are modest. Except for a family vegetable garden, he never works the land or intends to, but he relishes his large, overgrown plot and above all, his barn. "That is where he keeps his *things*," said Kenya to me. Whoops, trouble. Whatever *things* she was referring to, it was already clear that she wants them atomized. Lars, it turns out, had extensive collections of stuff, old stuff that a person finds at country auctions or estate sales: turntables, piano rolls, horseshoes, kerosene lamps, Sears catalogues, magazines, more magazines and pot-bellied stoves. "And the home for all of his things is his *hulking barn*," said Kenya.

As a young man Lars had been exceptionally busy as an auctioneer in territory that included the southern half of Minnesota and spilled over into Iowa and Wisconsin. That's how Kenya found him. Looking for bargains to furnish her first apartment, she attended a large auction near the rural town of Norseland. As Kenya watched Lars rattling words on that platform, she became captivated by his command of the scene, by his brawny shoulders and by that shock of straw-colored hair. After the auction she loitered until she caught his eye, then flirted with him. "Mercilessly," she said. He didn't seem to mind, and they married a year or two later.

At first Kenya paid little heed to the barn. After all, Lars' plot afforded them a house with no mortgage, and although it was definitely in the countryside, she had a convenient half-hour drive to her job in Minneapolis. In fact, she forgot about the barn and overlooked the fact that Lars kept increasing its inventory for no apparent or useful reason. When the children were small, it was a perilous playground, so Kenya kept them away from its temptations. As they grew, they ambled in by themselves and sometimes became intrigued with a gramophone or broken accordion.

Although she rarely visited the barn, occasionally Kenya would fetch Lars there if none of the children was around to do it. But over the years she developed a growing sense of panic as she approached the place. Lars' things seemed to be reproducing. A herd of rusting tractors grazed outside along with loaders, spreaders and other farm implements, alien and obsolete. Inside milking stools, rocking chairs and weather vanes hung from rafters in precarious suspension; cupboards, washstands and pig troughs teetered in uneasy towers; bee hives, milk churns and rolls of bale wrap cluttered corners; canning jars, tin cups, bowling pins, false teeth and snake oil filled trunks and barrels.

Kenya began to manage her panic with denial, a handy but short-sighted strategy. She bought a cell phone to reach Lars in the barn and stopped showing the place to family and friends, even the ones who were junk aficionados. But her denial wore thin—she wasn't very good at it—and one day when her friend Deb was visiting, it disappeared altogether. She found herself disgorging her frustrations and fears about the barn and all of its ramifications: "We need money, Deb. Teenagers are expensive, and Jenn will be going off to college in less than two years. How will we pay for it? Lars won't get a regular job because he thinks he has one: taking care of his stuff. But he never sells any of it. My god, you'd think these things were his children. He *names* them." Kenya paused. She'd said more than she had intended. "Please … please, don't tell anyone. He has a wheelbarrow he calls Rusty, a milk churn named Daisy and … I can't stand it … a pickle crock named Sweet Gherkin. And we need cash."

"Let's have a look," said Deb.

"You go," said Kenya, "and report back to me." So Deb walked up to the barn, said hello to Lars who was repairing a porch swing, politely looked around, inquired about a few curios, then returned to the house.

Deb, who writes advertising copy, nailed the essence of the scene: "It's the Detritus of Armageddon." Kenya wept in her arms. She had married the bartender who is trapped by drink.

On the advice of Deb, Kenya again asked Lars to have his own auction; she begged, hounded and cajoled him. For months. He said he wasn't ready and after all, he still had ample room for storage. His growing interest in eBay briefly offered some hope, but he would post one sorry item at a time, then proudly announce its sale to Kenya. Her response: "And that leaves only 15,698 more items," just a little sarcasm she reserved until the kids were out of earshot. He stopped celebrating his sales with her.

At this point, the reader may be wondering why Kenya puts up with Lars. After all, she is a successful professional woman who can conjure up enough spit and fire to get along on her own. This is why: she counts him as a great dad, he does all of the cooking and grocery shopping and he is a cheerful, accommodating lover. But because he pulls his weight in these ways, he doesn't think that he owes much in terms of family income. For most of their marriage, Kenya had more or less agreed with that. Even now, he still works an occasional auction, and he *is* a landowner. "It's not Tara, but it has its own kind of dignity," he says.

Tara didn't last for reasons of its own, but Lars is determined that his estate will face a different fate. However, as Kenya and Lars' children have been growing, so has a threat to his property. A suburb has sprouted, matured and now encircles them. As it began encroaching more than a decade ago, developers offered to buy Lars' land. Of course, you know the fate of the barn if that were to happen. Developers have no respect for barns, and no one knows it better than Lars. From the start he has shunned them and stood as lonely as the town leper. Nevertheless, living on their little island, the family has all the conveniences of modern life. They are located just under a mile from Chili's on Franchise Row where Kenya and Lars occasionally sit on tall stools, eat designer enchiladas and sip banana-mango margaritas. Lars doesn't much like Chili's, but he recognizes the benefits of appeasing Kenya, with her urban and suburban tastes.

Lars' time, however, was running out, and that kind of appeasement, like the eBay sales, was becoming too paltry to count for much with Kenya. One night as she perched on one of the tall stools, she became hawkish: "Look, Jenn's going to college in less than two years. Ben and Rob will be right behind her. How are we going to pay for it? Our property taxes are outrageous, and we can no longer afford the land. If we sell it, we'll have more than we need to pay for their educations. *I want you to sell our land.*"

Lars blanched. "Not the barn."

"Yes, the barn. The whole bundle."

"Not the barn."

"Yes, all of that junk and that hulking, looming, god-damned, ill-begotten barn!"

Caught licking their salty lips, fellow margarita sippers jerked their heads in the couple's direction, but Kenya did not back down. The disputed barn held them in a paralyzed stand-off for several weeks until the day Kenya called FABRCTR.

For months I worked with the couple. They live with multiple differences, differences which are both troubling and complementary. She loves the life of the city and her work in advertising. Lars takes care of the domestic demands and his property where he can live in a world that still feels spacious, accommodating and filled with the past—all too literally. Even I could see that there was value for him in these things, but Kenya had ceased to see it. She gathered together all of her resentments as exhaustively as Lars had gathered his collectibles. All of our discussions rotated back to the same deadlock: Sell the property vs. keep the property.

If that wasn't discouraging enough, I got blindsided by this case. My husband Jake is also a collector of ponderous proportions. One day I finally said to the man, "It's that stuff or me, not both." Well, we worked it out a few decades ago—I'll tell you about that later—but now it was feeling as fresh as a tomato just plucked from its stalk. I did stop short of telling Lars that he had to choose, and my team gave me some advice: "You're not Kenya," Regis-Rittenhouse said. "It's her business what she wants to say. Besides it's the money, not the stuff that is the sticking point. Hold your tongue." I did, but my it was bloody from restraint.

Yes, the money is the bugaboo; the rest is clutter. The issue seemed as irreconcilable to us as it was to them. Kenya had put up with too much for too long, and now she was nearly done. Bloom wrung her hands: "How can we help this couple? Differences, differences, money differences. It's breaking them up." Sack was silent, not always a good sign although sometimes it means that something is percolating. And it was. "The kids," he said. "Get the kids in."

The couple was skeptical when I suggested it, but I said, "What's to lose? We'll get their take on it." So they brought the three teenagers to the church—fortunately none of them was surly—and each had plenty to say. After a warm-up, I slipped them a question: "What do you guys think of the barn?"

"It, like, embarrasses me," said Jenn. "My friends seriously think I live on a farm, and, like, we're so totally not farmers or pioneers or anything. But, you know, that's … just Dad. He's, like, way weird, but he's my dad."

And Ben: "Cool. Dad's stuff is cool But what are you gonna do with it, Dad? Sometimes I wake up in the middle of the night and wonder about it: What's gonna happen to Dad's stuff?"

And Robbie: "Let's sell all the stuff except for the turntables. Dad, we need to face it, eBay is too slow. We can have a gigantic auction and everybody will come and we'll serve lemonade and play hip music and make some money. And we'll call it the Great Suburban Get-Together."

Following the family meeting, Lars spent a few agonizing months coming to terms with the impending loss of his trove.

Eventually, he couldn't resist the pull of his family's energy for the Great Suburban Get-together. When the day arrived, Kenya watched as Lars called bids and saw the young straw-haired man who had once captivated her. She warmed to him and might have felt guilty when she saw him wince as an ornamental barrel named Fancy Fats was sold, but giddiness edged out her guilt. Although he was disappointed that many of his treasures were underappreciated and practically given away, others sold beyond expectations.

Everything went but for one pot-bellied stove which Lars kept for himself and four turntables for Robbie who apparently sees some future for himself in them. The event produced enough college money for Jenn's first year or two. However, the strip-mined barn still stands, and developers are still stalking the place.

END OF CASE

"Money," said Sack. "Only sex is more complicated."

"What?" I asked. "I thought you said … Never mind."

Our team agreed that the case had been a success and that Sack had been a key player. This couple's work in settling differences is not over, but the junk problem and the financial crunch are temporarily moderated. I had thought that the cavernous barn would likely lose its pull on Lars. But not. Just after their last visit, he told me *sotto voce*—and there was no need because Kenya was in the bathroom down the hall—that he had begun collecting again so maybe he'd have another auction in a few years. And he invited me to come. (I think I'm busy that day.)

"Pru, they'll be back in a year or two," said Sack. I know.

In an attempt to be hopeful, Bloom capped our work on differences with this hopeless observation: "Marriage to either a clone or identical twin would eliminate the problem of dissimilarities."

"Those marriages could never be heterosexual and that's what most people want," said Regis-Rittenhouse. "Besides, cloning humans is illegal and so is marrying one's twin, at least in most states, and even if that weren't the case, all of the neighbors of these misbegotten souls would shun them, maybe even cast stones. Anyway, no one has found any pair of identical twins who want to marry one another." Even Bloom appreciates the incisive Regis-Rittenhouse take on these matters.

Chapter II

TALKING, LISTENING AND OTHER DUBIOUS FORMS OF COMMUNICATION

In the beginning people grunted and they still grunt. Like the hammer, the grunt never disappeared but has been adapted, sometimes disguised, updated and put to hundreds of uses, some of them nefarious. The same may be said for other vocal emissions, most notably talking. Just when the grunt morphed into the word is not altogether clear, and whether that word was listened to is even less clear. Although talking and listening are considered the yin and yang of communication, they do not necessarily occur together. The assumption that when someone talks someone else is listening trips up a seriously large percentage of our couples. Communications more likely to be noticed are grimaces, long-suffering sighs, winks, whistles, kisses and stonewalling.

Talking remains surprisingly popular in marriages, however, even though it often leads to semantic quagmires, locked horns and tearful fiascos. It is less popular among certain peoples of Northern European extraction who are known to get along with fcw words, but these people, often farmers, are a dwindling minority in this country. And Eastern sages, who are disinterested in explaining things, also escape the encumbrance of words, but Eastern non-sages and humans in general exhibit a remarkable aptitude and passion for all forms of talking and not just explaining, but consoling, boasting, twaddling, praising, whining, placating, hectoring, carping, reassuring and gossiping, especially gossiping.

Our team knew that we could not avoid the ubiquitous issue of the word. When we assembled for an exploratory meeting on communication research, however, the prevalent mood was boredom with a dash of disgust. That dash came from Regis-Rittenhouse who said that the topic had been overworked and trivialized. She broke into a little sociodrama:

"You don't care about me anymore." (High, squeaky voice)

"Of course, I care about you." (Deep, resonant voice)

"Oh, Honey, I'm so glad we can talk about it this way. We never could have done it if we hadn't read together *Every Couple's 5-Step Guide to Heaven-Sent Communication*." (High, squeaky voice)

Her performance was slightly energizing for us and we suspected that once again FABRCTR would be on the cutting edge of something. For one thing, we knew what to avoid because we can learn from other people's mistakes. The active listening trend is over. Hardly anyone even does it, certainly not happy couples. Venting anger is out and conflict avoidance is a draw: Some couples avoid conflict, others rise to a fevered pitch. Whatever works. If they must, we are told, women can criticize but should do so in a calm, gentle manner. Men apparently don't criticize (except for the men I know). Nope, our group would not touch any of these communication issues. They are cooked.

Only Bloom was not quite up to speed on this. She wanted some research that examined the effects of couples saying hopeful things to one another.

"Like what?" Dopplemann asked.

"Well, like, I don't know … like, 'Our love will see us through,'" Bloom answered. Regis-Rittenhouse rolled her eyes.

Sack was doubtful that we could study couple communication at all. He did not trust that anything couples say or do in front of their marriage therapists authentically represents what they do in private. He had a point; it's unlikely that they actually become unbuttoned before our eyes. But he lost us with his reminder that the Heisenberg Uncertainty Principle says that there is no observer outside of the experiment. Doppelmann yawned. Bloom concentrated on her cross-stitching. "So if infinitesimal particles are affected by an observer, what does that say about the effect of a marriage counselor who is sitting right there?" Everyone appeared thoughtful.

"Nothing," Regis-Rittenhouse said.

"And here's another confounding variable," Sack said. "It's what people don't say that is meaningful and profound, like at night … lying in bed in dead silence with someone who doesn't understand your reality. Who ever talks about that?" (Actually, Sack does. And I suspected that he was lying in bed those nights with his dog Hobbes, and we were reasonably certain that Hobbes did not understand Sack's reality, but then neither did his wife, and we were not doing much with his reality right then either.)

Apparently overdosed on Mountain Dew again—it keeps him propped up during his gloomy times—Sack was not to be discouraged by his failure to rouse us and kept steaming along. He described one of his couples who fought with silence. After a contentious, unresolved dispute, they could go weeks without saying a word to one another while maintaining their favorite activity, Scrabble. A mutually stubborn couple, neither wanted to yield their position or to sacrifice a beloved pastime. The message was this: "I will stick around even though I am incontrovertibly right and you're irrational and illogical. But you're a decent Scrabble partner." No one had to say it.

Sack settled down after no one disagreed with his contention that the absence of the spoken word can be a powerful form of communication. That was fine, but we needed a little order and direction, so as the FABRCTR scribe, I pointed out that the topic of communication is too ungainly and suggested that we narrow it down, preferably to forms which have been neglected, misrepresented or unfairly maligned in the marital literature. "Too many valuable uses of the language have been overlooked," I added. "And the tormenting nature of others has been insufficiently addressed." We haggled a little before everyone concurred that we share our collective wisdom and experience with the reader regarding a handful of judiciously chosen verbal exchange modes. After an hour or so of free-range dialogue, we discarded—regretfully—several ripe possibilities and settled on even riper ones: Bargaining, bloviation, eye rolling, faint praise, gossip, lectures (and sermons), nagging, nattering, singing and storytelling. No foof dust for us. No, this would be a guide for couples who want direction in red-blooded real talk.

Quick Guide to Real Talk

Bargaining: The value of bargaining in your relationship cannot be overstated. Wrangle, haggle, underbid, negotiate, barter and settle. Trade kitchen patrol for homework supervision, trade a visit to your in-laws for a Spider-Man movie, trade sex for a good conversation, trade your car for a trip to Paris. And make it clear. Bloom thought our concept of couple bargaining was cynical, but we reminded her that every relationship is inherently a deal. "Even an inveterate romantic like Doppelmann understands this," I said.

Bloviation: Although this sounds like it might be a bovine activity, cows never engage in bloviation. Bragging and boasting is, for better or worse, exclusively human (although the peacock with that excessive fan on its posterior may be exercising this behavior in some primitive form). Before marriage bloviation may be necessary, but after marriage it has mixed results. Some relationships allow it the way they allow belching: They have a contract that the behavior is acceptable between the two of them but not in front of other people. In public they may be able to offer a healthy check and balance for one another to prevent social embarrassment, but unfortunately couples can lapse into a bloviation team and fail to notice that the smiles on their listeners are pasted on or that a tactful scattering of listeners often ensues.

Eye Rolling: Although eye rolling is not a verbal behavior, it nevertheless holds a significant place in the realm of couple communication. Best done when your partner is out of eye-shot, it is a way to express yourself without being heard. Do this instead of saying the riskier "Not this again" or "Give me a break" or "That is the most f**ked-up idea I have ever heard in my life." A roll of the eyes actually spotted by your partner invites ill humor. And if he or she has a hair-trigger temper, you might as well be hurling a hand grenade.

Faint Praise: At first our group thought that we might find some merit in faint praise, but we found none. One woman whom I counseled recounted her holiday experience: After she had spent two days putting together a Thanksgiving feast, served her guests, cleaned the kitchen, and tossed out the turkey carcass, her partner said, "Well, the bird wasn't too dry this year." A jail sentence is not enough. Subject the man to five years of sensitivity training.

Regis-Rittenhouse aptly summarized our feelings about faint praise: "Put it through the shredder."

Gossip: This is a grand form of communication. It can hold whole societies together, and if both partners share a zest for it, does an adequate job for marriages as well. Keeping up on national and international gossip, just a click or two away, takes no talent really, maybe a little curiosity, although it is enough for some couples. Local gossip is more intriguing and the closer to home, the better. Excellent sources are your workplace, church, synagogue, mosque, yoga center or whatever, and best of all, your neighbors. Couples often bond keeping an eye on them. Few of us will ever share with our partners the likes of a *Rear Window* experience because we will not have a neighbor who murders and dismembers his spouse, but we sure would be interested if we did. However, lesser dramas will do. Parties provide an excellent peeping event. Peer through your window and check out who comes, who goes, what kind of vehicles they drive, how late it lasts, whether you should be grateful or indignant not to be invited, and whether the police show up. Then put it all together and decide what kind of people your neighbors are.

If you live in a flimsy apartment building, endless information can be had. Listening to quarrels through the heating ducts is entertaining, less so the bed bumping rhythmically against your wall for most of a weekend. Music savvy can be evaluated, garbage surveyed and cooking odors sniffed: "Phew! It may be Chinese, but thank god it's not what we eat at The Mandarin Kitchen." High rises, flimsy or substantial, provide an elevator culture where you can learn a lot about the backsides of people, get a glimpse of their front sides, exchange weather information and use all of it to piece their lives together. "Who's the dude in the purple sweats? The one who jogs in any weather, even during thunderstorms. ... He lives with that woman with the medusa hair? My god, she's ancient. ... No, I don't think he's her son."

Some couples discuss these things interminably and as long as they are discreet, there is no harm in it. They may merely be entertaining themselves or they may be underlining their togetherness through a perceived common enemy. Men who put too much stock in their manliness may pretend as though they are not interested, but if you watch closely, you will detect a subtle lifting of the left eyebrow when you share a delicious bit of neighborhood gossip with him.

Lecturing and Sermonizing: Within a marriage, lecturing is a form of communication especially vulnerable to listener ennui. This is especially true if it is a repeated lecture. His eyes glaze over and you don't notice because you are too caught up in your own brilliance and your lucid grasp of the issue. While there is nothing inherently wrong with a lecture, it easily slips into condescension. People prone to lecturing generally know much less than they think they do, so if you are the lecturee (see Glossary), you may not want to believe everything you hear. Those who do it professionally, such as college professors, are usually discerning enough to refrain from lecturing at home, but not always. Sermons are worse than lectures because they have moral overtones, which makes the sermonizer somewhat suspect.

Nagging: The repetitious nature of nagging can be reassuring for any couple who believes that things are going badly. Like the neighborhood garbage truck that makes the rounds every Tuesday at 6 or 7 AM, it deludes you into thinking that all is well and that what happens next is a foregone conclusion: Your garbage will be dumped in some faraway place that you will never see and don't have to think about, and then you will get in your car and drive to work. So too, nagging. Compare this scenario: One partner comes in and drops his jacket on the floor. Soon he hears, "Yananana … jacket … floor … yananana … How many times … yananana?" He may pick up his jacket or he may not, but that isn't the issue; the issue is that life will go on as usual. If the nagging partner does not mention the jacket, what happens next is not a foregone conclusion. He worries: Maybe she has given up on me, maybe she is having an affair, maybe she is hatching some treacherous plot against me. Her oversight is disturbing because it clouds the future. With enough fissures such as this, a marriage could collapse. Our team agrees that nagging is a form of communication with some constructive elements.[2]

Nattering: Occasionally, a member of our team sees a couple with one partner who talks incessantly. Sack admits to cowering in the face of it, Bloom frets, Regis-Rittenhouse says, "You talk too damn much," I say the same thing, but without the damn, and Doppelmann fades into his fantasy world. We have speculated that the nattering woman—and I regret to say that it's nearly always a woman—is releasing anxiety, that her every scrap of anguish about the mysteries of pain, death and destruction follow some labyrinthian trail through her body until they transform into an unfortunate, extended vocalization about the dandruff on her husband's shirt.

Curiously, most of the husbands of these women have a bemused, almost Zen-like countenance during the disgorgement. When we have asked them how they feel about it, they usually just shrug a little. If these women don't annoy their husbands, why should Sack, Bloom, Regis-Rittenhouse and I care? Our group decided that Doppelmann has it right. As a result of our discussion, the rest of us have shed our worry about the natter matter.

Singing: Although singing is not technically a form of talking, we do not apologize for using it in our Real Talk guide. We think of it as celestial in nature, a form of word usage sadly overlooked in many marriages, perhaps because one of the

---

[2]Feedback from the reader on this or any of our other insights is welcome at FABRCTR5@gmail.com.

partners sings off-key. If this is your reasoning, we implore you to reconsider. Along with whistling, it can communicate joy and contentment. As agreeable as singing can be, however, it has its hazards. As previously mentioned, our receptionist Holly attempts to renew hope for couples who have lost it with bits from the score of *Camelot*. The most hopeless of the waiting-room crowd, however, become dismayed by the words, "One brief shining moment." They rush to judgment, believing that their moment has come and gone. Holly then must explain to them that they should not take the lyrics quite so literally, that they're likely to have many brief shining moments. Once a couple, complaining that they expected many shining years, not just moments, left during her explanation and before even seeing a marriage counselor. That was a bad day for Holly who nearly resigned in disgrace, but we reassured her that any couple who expected so much would never have made it anyway. For the others, we recommended a song with less ambiguous lyrics, maybe *"Don't Worry, Be Happy."* On the whole, however, we believe that sharing a song like sharing a meal has primal appeal for any couple.

Storytelling: And finally, there is storytelling which we admit converges with gossip. A story you tell your partner does not have to be true, but it is prudent to let your partner know this if it is not readily apparent. Make it interesting and spin it a little if you must. If it is a familiar story, one that you have repeated many times, the listener can just relax and move into her own fantasies which may have more variety and better characters than your story. Good stories make good partners.

END OF GUIDE

Doppelmann said that these descriptions might be helpful for our readers, but that so far our discussion and conclusions had put too much emphasis on vocal emissions and too little on context and location. "Regardless of what these people are saying, we need to see where they are when they communicate, to follow them from room to room, outside and down the block. Do they just follow each other around, huddle in the bathroom or nestle on the couch? Or are they too far away from each other to be heard? I'll bet that they just ramble around."

None of us was immediately certain whether or not Doppelmann had a cogent point about the significance of location and context in couple communication, so in our customary democratic style, we talked it through. I noted that I had sometimes found myself imploring a client to stop yelling, come in from the garage, turn off the dishwasher and talk face-to-face with his partner. Sometimes he will go home and do it, sometimes not. Maybe this behavior is so difficult to snuff out because of his general ambivalence about communicating, because he is miffed with his wife just then, because he is all wrapped up in the fuel line or because he is just lazy. If he could not tell me, how could I divine it from my office? I agreed with Doppelmann that we just might be able to discover the underlying reasons for this behavior by observing couples at home.

Regis-Rittenhouse resisted. "Doppelmann, you just want to get into people's houses," she said. The group had a little go-around about that, but we finally concurred that his idea had merit, and Sack seemed to forget about the Heisenberg Principle for the time being. No other group had done research shadowing couples to track their conversations in situ.

41

Regis-Rittenhouse agreed to design the study and analyze the results. Because couples have often asked that we accompany them home to see what happens there, to help them manage their quarrels on the spot or to provide them with ongoing reassurance, we were not surprised that so many were willing to be part of this study. Several of them also requested that we follow them outside of their homes too because they often talked or even came to blows while walking the dog or eating at the deli. We did not, of course, tell them about our area of concentration because we wanted them just to move about as they normally would.

Peregrination Study

Each of us tracked ten couples and recorded their peregrinations, moods and verbal exchanges. Data gathering was not without its complications. At first Bloom had difficulty concentrating because she kept wiping sticky kitchen counters and comforting crabby babies, small children or an occasional teenager. Her work improved when we assigned her to homes without these distractions, but it was tricky to tell in advance just which couples were likely to have sticky kitchen counters. Doppelmann and Regis-Rittenhouse were each bitten once by a family dog, and I became quite unstrung by the sudden appearance of a pet Gila monster. (People should keep their Gila monsters in cages. The owners said it had been detoxified, but nevertheless.) Otherwise, our work went fairly smoothly.

After the data had been gathered, Doppelmann was so eager to see the analysis that he pestered Regis-Rittenhouse until she locked him out of her office. When she completed the task, she presented us with the results which described six basic patterns of movement during couple communication:

Stairwells: These are the busiest couples. They talk or argue in hallways and stairwells. Usually at least one of them is carrying a child, a basket of laundry or a pizza box. We liken these couples to the pioneers who were too busy to worry about talking and listening because they were working the land and churning the butter. Although talking had been around for millenniums, they did not have time to dwell on the nuances. And neither do the Stairwells. Sometimes this works in their favor.

Kitchen Sinks: These couples talk while pacing around the counters, the stove, the trash compactor and the refrigerator. They talked the most of any of the groups and they talked about everything, everything *and* the proverbial kitchen sink. We all agree that they talk too much and it was tedious, at least for the researchers. Any nagging that occurs is most likely to happen here (The second most likely location is a family vehicle unless it's a motorcycle.) Controversy over the crumbs in the butter dish and peanut butter on the refrigerator handle is common. Bloom's families were more likely to be Kitchen Sinks than those of the rest of us, and here we must admit to the possibility of flawed data. Her couples probably hung around the kitchen because they knew she would tidy up. Regis-Rittenhouse also pointed out that Bloom's Kitchen Sink couples received higher ratings on the Sanguine Scale. More than likely her assistance reduced their stress and promoted a sense of well-being. (She did suggest to three or four couples that they hire someone to clean and was flattered when offered the position in two households. She declined.)

Ramblers: These couples move around a lot during their conversations. Maintaining a constant flow of words, they follow one another into the yard, down to the mailbox and into the bathroom. With some notable exceptions, this group is the most congenial, although sometimes one of them wants to be alone and has to spit fire to get the other one off his trail. Doppelmann found several of these couples, thus confirming his own hypothesis that couples are inclined to move around when they talk. The rest of us found fewer wandering couples, although we noticed the salutary effect of wandering on marriage and recommend that more couples try it.

Bunkmates: These couples do most of their talking and arguing in bed. Our data gathering was a little different with this group. Out of respect for their privacy, we did not accompany them into their bedrooms, but with their permission, we wired their rooms so we could listen down the hall. On the whole, these couples were very sweet to one another, although I am chagrined to report that a few of them saved their most vicious attacks for this darkened space. Sack found more Bunkmates than the rest of us did.

Far Cries: This is the most pathetic type. The Far Cries attempt to communicate while in different parts of the house or apartment, which causes frequent accusations of deafness. Sometimes one of their children will intervene. A daughter may travel from the attic where her mother is looking for a Halloween costume to the basement where her father is operating a buzz saw and the radio is blaring a Vikings' game to tell him that mom is talking to him and ask why he isn't listening to her. (Bloom became quite distressed about parents asking children for these favors and would instruct them to go outside and play in the sandbox.) Cell phones have helped couples in some cases; however, others will not use them, apparently because they prefer a perpetual state of disjunction.

Smorgasbords: These couples do most of their talking at meals. The emotional range is as variable as the table fare. A tetchy partner may take this opportunity to trap his partner into listening while he disgorges his complaints, disappointments, criticism and regrets or to goad a child into eating food that she not only finds disgusting, but is convinced will lead to sudden death A romantic partner, on the other hand, may savor the eyes of his mate, the bouquet of the wine and the tang of the sauce. But unfortunately few of our families sat down to the table at all. On the whole those who did often talked with reasonably good cheer and talked of many things, of cabbages and kings.

END OF STUDY

The astute reader may note that television is not mentioned in any of our identified patterns of movement during couple communication. This is because conversations rarely take place in front of an operating TV set. If someone does talk there, it goes poorly. The exception, of course, is televised sporting events where utterances are not only allowed but welcomed and sometimes even required as long as the viewer supports the chosen team and mimics its fans. Jingo, jungle noise.

When all was said and done, Regis-Rittenhouse said she thought that our research was a testament to meager ambitions, that it could not be considered serious research and that among other things, observer bias affected the outcome. "That's what I was trying to say in the first place," said Sack. Doppelmann could not be discouraged and must have forgotten his own eloquent words on the salience of mystery in marriage when he proclaimed, "This is a bold and daring study. It demystifies the entire realm of couple communication." Bloom and I thought it might have some promise for future investigations.

Chapter III

MIND READING AND OTHER PARANORMAL PHENOMENA

So listening and talking aren't all they're cracked up to be. And sometimes even a single spoken word can mean so many things that it is rendered as useless as a bottomless pocket. Open your dictionary. The first definition of the word love begins in heaven—a *profoundly tender, passionate feeling for another person*—then rambles on in tiny print for almost two inches as its various meanings become increasingly disappointing and reach a nadir at number eleven: *a score of zero in tennis.* So much for love. At other times, a cluster of words is simply lost between two people—snipped and swept away like wisps of hair in a barber shop. But even if words do materialize within earshot, have sufficient staying power and carry a shared meaning, they can lead to confusion or conflict. Except for gossip, marriage might be well rid of them.

We began with a tactical, idea-generating meeting on the subject of alternatives to words. Very shortly, out of the corner of my eye, I could see Doppelmann lighting up. Reaching full candescence all too soon, he exclaimed that he wanted to break the bonds of karma: "Let's hire a Zen Buddhist and study Eastern mysticism to free our minds from words and explanations." He elaborated, Bloom fidgeted—she had forgotten her cross-stitching—Sack worked a hangnail and Regis-Rittenhouse erupted: "Doppelmann, this is just a ploy to dress up. You envision yourself in loose, flowing garb while entrancing a collection of reverent, lost souls with your deep spiritual wisdom. It's been done. Forget it." No one came to Doppelmann's rescue, and with only a slight hint of deflation, he dropped the idea. (I expect that he will resurrect it in the future.)

As it turned out, Sack had more in mind than his hangnail. He was off on a riverbank hatching an idea. As though he were pulling words out of some primordial ooze, he said, "Mind reading … mind reading." We all paused thoughtfully and it seemed that our minds locked for an instant. Even Doppelmann, re-inhabiting his indigo sweater, joined the lock. Of course. Why hadn't we thought of it before? We were frequently bumping up against people's obstinate, misguided confidence in their own mind reading skills. Let's take the Littles again. Some notion about Hank's motive for depositing his shoes on the living room floor just pops into the head of Traci who immediately transforms her notion into this fact: He is angry that her sister Susi and boyfriend are coming to live with them again and is too passive-aggressive to admit it. Hank, who has been just plain sloppy about his clothes since he was a toddler, is rendered powerless over this freshly formulated fact because he isn't told what it is, but even if he were, once present in Traci's mind, it is like head lice, the extraction of which is a convoluted, protracted and ignoble process. Sack had nailed it; he pinpointed a mental activity sorely neglected in the marital literature, an activity that touches the angst of relationships universally: longing, delusion, grandiosity, anger, denial, disappointment and fear. A goldmine.

The mind-lock instant disappeared and each of us followed our own trajectory, that is, we all became self-absorbed. Sack said he considered himself a fairly skillful mind reader which prompted Regis-Rittenhouse to ask him, if that were the case, why had he been so thoroughly dumbfounded by Shirley's departure. He returned to his hangnail while Bloom and Doppelmann, apparently heedless of the risk, each offered themselves some self-congratulation along the same lines. I was tempted to brag a little myself, but this looked like a party I didn't quite want to join. Regis-Rittenhouse pulled the puffery right out from under all of us. "You are delusional," she said. "When people think they are reading minds, they are actually reading slouched shoulders, raised eyebrows, busy fingers, long pauses, razor-sharp stares or more pathetic still, they are just navel-gazing. Yes, navel-gazing. They make this stuff up whether their partner is around or not. For god's sake, one of them could be in Alaska, the other in Argentina, and both obsessively mind reading. Hapless, delusional souls. With a partner, we mind read what they are mind reading we are mind reading they are mind reading. Look." In fast forward she drew diagrams on the whiteboard. "See, this is how you imagine it goes. One way, clear and simple. And, of course, the mind reader has complete confidence that he is accurately perceiving the truth."

Figure 1. Regis-Rittenhouse view of a typical domestic-partner mind-reading delusion at the end of a workday.

"But you know what? This is how it really goes."

Figure 2. Regis-Rittenhouse view of typical domestic-partner mind-reading cross-miscalculations at the end of a work day.

Regis-Rittenhouse was a little more reality-based than we wanted to be and closed-minded too. We told her so. Even hard science has found that two people close to one another might synchronize their heartbeats. Perhaps their minds do the same. Certainly besotted individuals are often convinced that their thoughts and feelings have merged with one another. But people well past the besotted stage can also become impressed with their own mind reading skills. Some of these individuals move into careers as palm readers, psychics, clairvoyants, past-life experts or ghostbusters. After discussing these endeavors and briefly considering them as potential career paths for ourselves, Bloom reminded us that as serious researchers, we must remain skeptical of these activities. We decided to limit our attention to standard domestic mind reading.

Over the next few months, we stayed alert to this issue. We found a jumble of attitudes, cleverly organized them and have doubtlessly become the first in the marital science field to develop a classification system for partner mind reading dispositions:

Sanguine-Confident Type: These individuals are absolutely convinced that they can read the minds of their partners and refuse to acknowledge error. Even when they are proved wrong, their confidence remains high.

Sanguine-Indifferent Type: These individuals claim never to have engaged in mind reading or, for that matter, thought much about it. (The reader is advised to remain skeptical because some members of this group may be dissembling.)

Vigilant-Agitated Type: These individuals are incessantly grazing for information about how their partners will fulfill their fantasies, expectations and desires. Typically, they *are using that information to calculate the most auspicious moment to make an amorous move.*

Vigilant-Shuttered Type: *These individuals fear that their partners actually have some mind reading skills and adjust their behavior accordingly.*

Crestfallen Type: *These individuals are deeply disappointed that their partners are incompetent mind readers.*

Relieved Type: *These individuals are deeply grateful that their partners are incompetent mind readers.*

With the accomplishment of the classification system behind us, we wondered what use to make of it. Of course, an identified Crestfallen, such as our Sack was before his separation, would need some help with accepting that he has a partner who is not even interested in what's on his mind. And perhaps he might learn to develop some social support to deal with loneliness, the risk being that no one else is interested in the contents of his mind either. A Vigilant-Agitated Type could be guided into broadening his interests, maybe developing another hobby because the use of one's partner as a hobby, that is, the focus of intense psychological and sexual inquiry, generally cracks the jar.

Bloom said that she didn't think our exploration would be complete without looking at couples who have spent decades together. She suggested that perhaps the longer people are together, the more effective they are at reading one another's minds. So we looked around for a coot and a crone. Most of the couples together 50 or more years had died off, finally divorced or moved to Florida. None of them came to FABRCTR, but Bloom had some neighbors, Harold and Ev, who have stayed put and weathered the seasons. In fact, Harold is out there every winter with his snowblower, his favorite toy. After a storm, he routinely clears the sidewalks on the entire block, which Bloom and Al appreciate. She called them to ask if they would be willing to come in. Harold answered and said that he and Ev would be honored to talk for the sake of research and that he'd check with the old gal right away about a time.

Harold and Ev

Now in their mid-eighties, Harold and Ev have been married for sixty-three years and have children, grandchildren and great-grandchildren scattered around the country. Retired for years, they live in a comfortable house with lots of lawn and, in the summer, a bed of petunias, daisies and black-eyed Susans. Bloom asked them about their retirement. "After Harold sold his business, we never moved to Florida or Arizona because we have so much to do here," said Ev. "We own a little lake cabin over in Wisconsin where we spend a lot of time in the summer."

"And that's plenty far to go," said Harold, "sixty miles or so. I can ice fish there in the winter and the two of us took up curl-in'—I have a little Scottish blood. So with that, plus the snow blowin', it's enough for me." Ev said that it's her preference to stay in St. Paul as well because her bridge group is here, and she still has a few piano pupils.

After gathering information for a meeting or two, Bloom decided to meet with each of them alone to see what they were up to on the mind reading front. She began with Harold and asked him about their daily life together. He said he gets up early, before Ev, reads the sports section, eats Cheerios and half a grapefruit, completes half of the crossword puzzle and stays trim. As far as Ev goes, he said, "Well, I don't have much to complain about. She's a good woman, but she didn't like the idea of movin' to Florida. 'Too many old people,' she says. I'da liked to do that. Ya know, marlin fishin'. But she's stuck on stayin' here, so that's why I got us into curlin'." Bloom pointed out that when they met together, he said he preferred staying here. "Well, ya know how it is, I don't want Evie to think I'm not happy with it. Why kick up the dust if ya don't have to? Let it lay. She doesn't much like arguments and after 63 years, ya get to know what a woman thinks. No sense arguin' about it."

Then Bloom met with Ev who fancies herself especially fluent in Haroldese. "He's transparent, Rose Ellen. I know that man like the back of my hand. Fortunately, we agree on most things, so we've had a pretty smooth go of it. But I wouldn't have minded moving to Florida. A few of our friends are in Sarasota, but he has no interest … seems to be pretty attached to the snowblower and the ice house. We don't have to talk about it. I've known him for so long. I just know that's how he feels, so why make a fuss? He doesn't like to argue."

Like Harold, Bloom saw no reason to mess with this, and after all, the couple had not come to change anything, just to help out. She thanked each of them for their participation, and they said they were pleased to do whatever they could to help couples who haven't been as lucky as they have been.

END OF CASE

Our group determined that this is either a mind reading failure of classic proportions or a mysterious anomaly. We considered what would happen if Bloom were to tell them that they both want to spend their winters in Florida. I suggested that rather than helping, it would be akin to bumping into a beehive. Pelted by a storm of hundreds of bees, all three would be instantly punished for clumsiness. Doppelmann couldn't resist a Pandora's Box riff: "Sixty-three years of regrets would come tumbling out." And so on.

Sack was at the top of his game. "Nope," he said, "no beehive, no box. Harold and Ev have been at this a long time. You point out that little crack in their wall, and they'll both have the spackle can and knife out in one minute flat. Add a little paint, the crack disappears and life goes on as usual." We agreed that if we can call their little stories mind reading, Harold and Ev would each be classified as the Sanguine-Confident Type, but what they are doing probably isn't mind reading at all, but subliminal agreements disguised as mind reading. Maybe that's what long-term married people just do.

Whatever Harold and Ev were doing, we had become convinced that the practice of mind reading would not be disappearing from the lives of couples anytime soon. As long as it is a given, like moist tongues and active imaginations, we reasoned, we may as well find some use for it. Recalling our experiences with communication between very busy partners, most notably the Stairwells who rarely have time to talk, we decided to explore the possibility of teaching mind reading as a shortcut in domestic communication. Perhaps, we speculated, we could develop an entire set of guides for skill-building, translate them into several languages and market them from Iceland to Fiji.

We decided to begin with the close scrutiny of a single case and chose the busiest couple we could find. The case belonged to Regis-Rittenhouse, a pleasant irony. She had substantially softened her views about mind reading since our initial discussion. (We suspected that she was currently dating someone. Doppelmann, our informant, had overheard her making plans on the phone *more than once*. People in relationships, fresh or highly ripened, become quite convinced of their genius for mind reading.)

Valerie and Chloe

After three dates, Valerie and Chloe had made the call: This was the relationship for them. They rented a truck and began a household: a blend of one golden retriever, one Welsh terrier, three Maine Coon cats, a cockatoo and themselves. Not only smitten with one another, they shared the dream of raising a rainbow family. Within four years they had adopted as many children: Guillermo, JinHee, Yolanda and Little Suleyman. Valerie had a thriving practice as a no-nonsense divorce attorney and worked 8–5. Chloe, an airplane mechanic, had the 3–11 shift. A nanny filled the afternoon gap. Otherwise, the children had the full attention of their very devoted parents. As luck would have it, Chloe shared her shift with a collection of dads who also stayed at home with their kids earlier in the day. During their breaks, they exchanged tips on diaper rash, toilet training and nutritious morning snacks.

Activities proliferated. Guillermo, whom they had adopted at five years old, was now eight and a gifted soccer player participating in two leagues. The moms enrolled JinHee in Korean, Yolanda in an African folk art class and Little Suleyman in Water Babies. And, of course, there were trips to the pediatrician, the dentist, the vet, the park, the zoo and Target. Valerie and Chloe were living their dream, but they never talked, not even in the stairwells. They left notes for one another, shopping lists, carpool schedules and appointment times. By the time they got to FABRCTR, they were near strangers. "Is that you, Chloc?" Valerie asked.

"I think so," her beleaguered partner answered.

Regis-Rittenhouse asked if they did any mind reading. All they could think of was their baby. When he whimpered or howled, they tried to read his mind. Because they seemed clueless about mind reading, she temporarily classified each as Sanguine-Indifferent Type. However, Regis-Rittenhouse was pushy enough to find out they were doing a lot of mind reading with one another. It just took her a while to fish it out.

Sex had evaporated with the arrival of Little Suleyman, the only child they had adopted as an infant. And it had not exactly been a thundering waterfall before that. Valerie was dead sure that Chloe no longer found her attractive. Chloe protested. Getting up with the baby—whom they were convinced was doomed to keep the hours of a racoon—was exhausting. Besides, Yolanda and JinHee usually crawled into bed with them sometime during the night. The animals also came and went, although the most introverted of the Maine Coons slept underneath the bed. And only recently had Guillermo excused himself. He decided that just babies and girls sleep with their moms, and being neither, he would stay in his own bed all night. Goldie, the retriever, joined him.

"Takeoffs and landings. Our bed is O'Hare Airport," said Chloe.

"You want all that traffic. It's a way to avoid our relationship."

"I just want some help with the traffic. Children and animals crawling all over and you're in the ultimate sleep zone. I'm the only controller on duty. Doesn't *anything* wake you up?"

"I thought you loved it."

Chloe didn't love it. She was exhausted and carrying a burdensome grudge. Valerie revealed a burdensome grudge of her own. She made all appointments, arranged carpools, handled soccer coaches and thoroughly prepared questions and complaints for teacher conferences.

"But you're so good at it, so charming, articulate, organized ... manipulative," protested Chloe. Valerie frowned. "Manipulative in a good way, I mean," Chloe further protested. "You are a scheduling genius and I deeply admire your abilities. In fact, you're a queen ... queen of the calendar." Chloe was losing ground fast. To save herself, "No, scratch that."

Even Regis-Rittenhouse wanted to leave, but persisted to rescue Chloe from her verbal briar patch. She was near tears and skirting frenzy. "See, I'm no good at this ... talking. I get too emotional, my tongue twists or my foot goes right into my mouth. Valerie is the one to do it. Can you imagine me trying to talk with those teachers and coaches? Without even meaning to, I'd insult them in minutes. Seconds." Her face fell into her hands, then gradually resurfaced pink and moist. She pleaded, "I can talk, but I just want to talk about kids out on the dock with the guys."

Regis-Rittenhouse, who had speculated that common gender would be an asset for effective mind reading, reassessed her view. And her plan to improve their skills only resulted in further failure. They were already doing their fair share of mind reading and doing it just as pathetically as straight people do. They did, however, make some progress with lip-reading which proved useful when the children were particularly boisterous. For several months she continued her work with Valerie and Chloe in the usual plodding ways. The moms

carved out a little time to be alone with one another, reluc-
tantly accepted one another's natural inclinations and settled
somewhat more comfortably into their makeshift domestic
roles.

END OF CASE

The FABRCTR team could think of no way around the efficiency of the spoken word, a handy little item. As riddled with
imperfections as it is, mind reading is worse. A vivid imagination is sometimes a welcome substitute for accuracy in the
daily grit of domestic duty, but more often your partner just
wants you to take out the garbage. (So get with it.) We may just
have to settle for the imprecision of words, of talking and of
listening until human clairvoyance evolves. Unlike ourselves,
animals seem to function remarkably well without talk,
but they rely heavily on instincts, odors and jungle noises,
resources which humans use less effectively. (We downplayed
the jungle discussion, however, because Doppelmann would
have had us doing research in the Amazon so he could outfit
himself in safari gear.) Regis-Rittenhouse had been right in
the first place: People read each other's behaviors, movements
and expressions, not their minds. Decoding of the forehead:
One furrow = quizzical; two furrows = annoyed; three furrows
= anguished. That's as good as it gets.

Chapter IV

SURVIVAL STRATEGIES: FORGETTING AND DISSEMBLING

Although forgetting and dissembling are assets for any marriage, they have their drawbacks. The main drawback of forgetting seems to be that partners do not forget the same things; of course, they do not remember the same things either. Taken together, these circumstances lead to quite divergent retrospectives of the relationship. One partner may remember the couple's first encounter in a cozy, quaint coffee house where she briefly glanced up from reading Proust to see a stranger with a lusty eye. He, on the other hand, remembers stepping into a shabby, misbegotten café and spotting some wild-haired woman reading pulp fiction, a woman who would give him no peace.

Accurate memory does not seem to be something that nature wants us to have. If so, there would be more of it. One problem is that memories dissipate. Sack says it's like radioactive half-lives. Half of the atoms in a substance decay in a given period of time, but no one can say which half decays and which half doesn't. And then it's just one half toppling after another until the substance is just a fragment left to eternally halve itself away. Meanwhile the vacated space fills up with something else, maybe shopping lists, baseball statistics, grand tales of one's own heroism and good works or just everyday emotional clutter.

Our team refers to this fill-in for forgotten moments and facts as *memory-by-proxy* (see Glossary). Except for the emotional clutter, memory-by-proxy serves us quite well. Like those little silver and gold nuggets in your teeth, the fill-in is often better than the old stuff. Not only that, but our partners do not seem to want us to have accurate memories because they can be quite threatening to the survival of the marriage. In an informal FABRCTR survey we found that 65% of marriages in which both partners have poor memories are successful, as opposed to only 30% in which they have fairly accurate memories. We have also observed that memory of the relationship deteriorates more rapidly in second and third marriages. Our speculation is that memory of prior marriages co-mingles with experiences in the current marriage and causes havoc in the already over-taxed human memory mechanism. (We have no data on fourth, fifth and sixth marriages, but we believe that the same principle applies.) Memory is not only distorted by prior marriages, but by mood-altering substances, stomach acid, headaches, movies, children, in-laws, shame, guilt and hormones. Especially hormones.[3]

When it comes to issues without emotional charge, a couple's divergent memories can be quite useful. For example,

---

[3]Doppelmann thinks there has been too much talk about hormones.

when one partner always remembers where the pliers are kept and another, the theater tickets, each becomes a key player and a sort of marital team spirit develops. Such spirit fails to emerge, however, if one of them misperceives that he is the only one who ever remembers anything.

Doppelmann didn't have much to say about forgetting because he was panting like a thirsty hound to get on to dissembling. He sees dissembling as one of the most intriguing and artful aspects of human beings. "It's man's greatest gift. Without it we would be arid, dull-witted creatures," he exclaimed. Bloom and I and even Regis-Rittenhouse overlooked Doppelmann's political incorrectness—he is a well-meaning man—and Sack reminded him that plants and animals are also great dissemblers (like the owl that looks like tree bark or the orchid that disguises itself as a female insect) and without that gift would be dead or extinct. But Doppelmann hardly lost a beat: "Yes, yes, all living things must dissemble. It's the quintessence of cleverness, the essence of vitality. Look no further than Shakespeare. He was a master dissembler, he and the great mystery man who actually wrote the plays. And those intriguing characters! They move about from one identity to another, just like their creator."

Doppelmann would have continued indefinitely, probably with a few Shakespearian subplots, then on to Oscar Wilde, but Bloom gracefully interrupted. "We need to remember that dissembling does have its disadvantages for the married," she said. Well, of course it has a poorer reputation than forgetting, but that reputation may be entirely unwarranted. Forgetting is more easily forgiven because it is often regarded as uninvited and unconscious, whereas dissembling is seen as manipulative and conscious. For the highly skilled dissemblers, it may be unconscious, but for those of us less accomplished, it takes a conscious, perhaps even a heroic effort. Sack, who admits to being a very poor dissembler, says he finds it exhausting.

And this is a problem for Sack and others because dissembling is critical to impression management. Married persons may exercise this skill individually and as a team. A couple who works as a team often has an exceedingly successful marriage unless it collapses under the weight of it, which it probably will if the dissembling becomes conscious. But unless a life crisis occurs or either one or both enter therapy, they will be fine. (We often advise against marriage counseling for the successful dissembling team.)

At the risk of disappointing Doppelmann, Regis-Rittenhouse apparently found it essential to proclaim that when it comes to dissembling, women have the evolutionary edge. She pointed out that historically women have had the misfortune of being too bright for their status and only survive as a gender because they have been especially gifted dissemblers. Bloom joined me in taking issue with her; we claimed that females have never been at risk of extinction and that if we did become extinct, men would disappear in unison with us. Regis-Rittenhouse, who does not brook being outdone, shifted her focus: "Even though males have usually served as the presidents and generals," she said, "women have covert power, but men don't seem to mind as long as it remains covert." Bloom agreed. So did Sack. In fact, Sack said that he didn't even mind if it was overt as long as the woman stays put.

As for our couples, many fail to see the advantages of forgetting and dissembling. Some of them, in a pitiful and misguided attempt to eliminate these behaviors, have installed surveillance cameras in their homes. Generally, this has failed to improve anything. If the filmed replay does not align with one partner's memory, that partner, obviously a poor sport, has been known to mumble, "Faulty film, who's been tampering ...? G**damn piece of junk. It goes back tomorrow."

Well, we knew we needed some cases for you, dear reader. Our ideas mean nothing if we cannot offer up some living, breathing, struggling couples to demonstrate our points. But as for forgetting and dissembling, we had as many relevant cases as Bartholomew Cubbins has hats. So we chose one highlighting what should be remembered, another, what should be forgotten, a third, what is purely fabricated and the last, what a gifted dissembler can do.

Markie and Matt

Bloom was treating Markie, a 27-year-old woman who had been quite content with her husband Matt at first, but after three years of marriage had grown bored with her life and, yes, probably with him. To liven things up, she enrolled in a jujitsu class where she developed an acute infatuation with her instructor, a fine figure of a man. Sight unseen, Bloom might have developed a little crush on him herself. (I thought she was tempted to go down to the jujitsu center and have a look, but she never actually said so. When I began writing this chapter, I asked her if she had felt the impulse. She couldn't remember.) Markie's attraction to the jujitsu instructor was mutual, the relationship heated up, an affair ensued, and then Markie remembered that her marriage had begun on shaky ground. Nearly 24 at the time, she feared that her prospects were dwindling month by month, and Matt was ready and waiting. Now she chided herself for her decision to marry him and breathlessly waited for her next tryst with the Body.

Her marriage had become frightfully dull, she reported to Bloom, because all she and Matt did together was to collect, polish and classify agates. Instead of seeking her own interests, she had joined him in his hobby in order to have a companionable marriage. They had an admirable agate collection for which they had recently captured a blue ribbon at the State Fair, but it had become increasingly tedious for Markie who was now feeling fire in her loins.[4]

After several months of marital deception, Markie's guilt was muscling in on her. She discussed it with Bloom for a few weeks running, then decided to tell Matt about the affair. After she did, the words toppled out. She said that there was no life left in their marriage, there never had been, agates totally bored her and she had found love and excitement in her jujitsu class. (She spared Matt the bitter news that the swain was her instructor.) Markie moved out. After a few weeks of shock, grief and anger, Matt called and asked her to come over because he was ready to discuss the agates and their marriage. When they were face-to-face, he said, "I don't care about agates. I thought that *you* wanted to do the agate thing. Remember? I gave you one while we were dating, and you loved it so much and declared it was so meaningful to you that you wanted to spend your whole life collecting agates with me. Remember? I

---

[4]Bloom wants me to inform the reader that this is just a little color that Doppelmann picked up from *Lolita* and that it has nothing at all to do with Bloom herself.

thought it was a little peculiar, but I figured, 'Agates, stamps, coins, what's the difference? We love each other.'"

Markie was stunned and shaken with incredulity. She had forgotten, completely forgotten, that he had once given her that agate. Did she ever actually love it ... or any agate? And why would they have carried on so long and so diligently with a bunch of stones? As she stared at Matt, her dim perceptions of the past rearranged themselves and came into focus; his face gradually became handsome again. And soft. And warm. And interesting.

At last report, Bloom said that Markie had dropped her jujitsu class as well as her instructor who said he was cool with it. The couple let the agate collection lie fallow, Matt started a collection of 45 rpms, and Markie tossed out her birth control pills.

END OF CASE

Whatever half life of a half life of a half life of Markie's memory that remained held at least a fragment of her early infatuation with Matt. Our team actually debated about whether or not to use this case to present to you because it could engender unwarranted hope. We do not want to be responsible for false expectations. The half life of a half life of a half life of your memory may not contain a shred of the infatuation you once had for your spouse, although it may contain more pragmatic aspects of your relationship. Perhaps you will remember that she earns more money than you do, that he is really good at finding his way around—much better than you—once outside of the county, that she is utterly intrepid when confronted with an overflowing toilet while you are a wuss or that your children will never talk to you again if you leave him. You would do well to remember all of these things.

Then there are the things that you would do well to forget. While Markie's memory needed tweaking, the memories of others need serious editing. Some modern readers of Proust have given up after the first hundred pages because the man remembered too damn much. Some people feel that way about their partners. I happened upon such a couple.

Celie and Lang

Celie, 38, has frizzy blonde hair and a broad, friendly smile. Lang, 46, is lean and lanky and stern. As soon as they began talking, her smile disappeared, but Lang's stern visage went nowhere. Married to him for 20 years, Celie said she could no longer live with a man who could remember every detail of her mistakes and misdemeanors. "He's brilliant; his memory is perfect. It's like a disease," she said. "He needs help with forgetting." And it was true. The more I heard, the more convinced I became that this man made a career—well, at the very least, a sustained hobby—out of Celie's every indiscretion, misstep and oversight. Worse, he had done the same with his children. At ages 19 and 20, they now lived out of the country. Celie said she knew why. Lang said it was because Celie had made so many blunders.

Now it was not tough to get a read on this guy, but getting that read across to him would be another matter. He was one impenetrable dude who somehow believed that a flawless memory entitled him to horsewhip his family. The real mystery was why Celie put up with him. Asking her did not elicit much more than a hem and a haw and, "Well, he doesn't drink or beat me." I thought a beer or two might be helpful and told him as much.

"It might rattle that memory, loosen it up, help you forget something," I said. He frowned.

Actually, I didn't see this case as being as hopeless as it may currently seem to you. I expected some crack to appear, some crack that I could wedge open. (My team expected the same.) And it did. It happened the day Celie mentioned that she wanted another clock in the kitchen, a request with such exaggerated significance for this couple that it immediately transformed my office into an emotional sauna. Aha. I did some of my best picking and poking and probing until Celie finally revealed that Lang had removed the batteries from the only clock there and had not allowed her or their children to replace them or to bring in another clock. Celie knew I wasn't going to give up until I got to the bottom of this, so she helped me out while the stone-faced Lang played statue. One evening twelve years ago she had arrived home at 6:20 PM.

Lang briefly broke pose: "Tell her why you were late."

"I'd gone to a bar with friends after work," said Celie. She was to have had dinner on the table twenty minutes earlier. Like Miss Havisham's aborted wedding, Celie's dalliance was permanently recorded on a clock, a clock frozen at 6:20 PM.

And that was just the tip of the elephant's tail. Neatly framed and hung above the living room couch were two concert tickets. These were tickets lost, then found three days after the concert. That bungle, of course, was attributed to Celie. A disembodied side-view car mirror dangled from the bathroom ceiling. Lang put it there after Celie, while backing the old Civic out of the garage, edged precariously close to the left, thereby knocking it off. The whole house was apparently done in Postmodern Botch. (Doppelmann was quite taken with the scene as I described it in case consultation. He envisioned these artifacts as Lang's trophies, like a stuffed wild boar or Arctic white fox in some hunter's drawing room.) In addition, Lang kept copious journals detailing each and every faux pas committed by their children and by the clueless Celie, who had been protecting him for far too long.

"Celie," I said, "if Lang's memory is so remarkable, why does he have to hang these things on walls, prop them on tables or write them down? These are all crib sheets." She was not eager to sacrifice the notion that she was married to a Mind, but she had brought Lang to FABRCTR, a move bound to have consequences. I told them to go home, gather up the clock, the side-view mirror, the journals and everything else that qualified as things-to-be-forgotten, invite the neighbors over and have a giant bonfire.

Of course, they didn't do it. Instead Celie tapped a vein of her own gumption—too long unmined—and came up with some mischief of her own. She began hanging Lang's dirty underwear—the stained pieces were the best—on household light fixtures. Gradually and mysteriously Lang's trophies and journals began to disappear.

END OF CASE

Marriage prospers when each of the partners judiciously forgets certain details and experiences. "And if not forgotten, a little tact will suffice," says Bloom. Our team recommends a little remembering, a little forgetting, all things in moderation. If Lang had ever even had it, he had lost his grip on this principle. It appears, however, that what he remembered actually did happen because Celie corroborated his accounts, more or less. In another kind of memory case, however, one partner remembers things that never occurred at all. We find examples of this outside of marriage too, so it can't be attributed solely to the despondency, discontent or disappointment within a relationship. For example, people are known to have seen James Cagney's fine performance in *The Godfather*, Marilyn Monroe's especially comedic performance in *9 to 5* and the Mad Hatter on Mulberry Street. For someone who is especially tied to one of these memories for whatever idiosyncratic reason, it is generally difficult to dispel and rarely worth the effort. When these cases occur with our couples, however, proof is often more difficult to find, but even if it is found, it may make no difference. As an example, we give you the Sack Flood Case.

Sally and Twitch

This couple presented at loggerheads about a flooded-basement memory. Twitch, 51, is a tall, lanky, congenial man and loose like a puppet. Sally, 50, is short, sweet and just a little intense. Both had grown up 40 miles northeast of St. Paul in a little river town where Twitch is now mayor.

What flapped their unflappability after nearly thirty years of marriage was Sally's memory of the flood of '92. It was nearly spring when the rising waters of the St. Croix River had crept onto their property and flooded the basement. She remembers it perfectly and in some detail. For example, she recalls that their dogs were hard to handle because they were constantly trying to sneak down for a swim, and if they were successful, which they were once or twice, they returned upstairs and shook themselves off, thereby casting a nasty spray across the kitchen floor. Spilled from an upended bin of old toys, saved for anticipated but as yet nonexistent grandchildren, were several plastic shovels and pails, colored balls and creatures which bobbed near floating coffee cans holding a few rusty nails or screws. The bath toys, especially the ducks and mermaids, added the perfect whimsical touch, Sally said. Gradually the water receded, the dogs thoroughly sniffed the place out, then lost interest, and the toys and cans settled randomly on the dank floor along with the rest of the detritus. Sally and Twitch cleaned it up. And what a clean-up it reportedly was.

"We bonded," Sally said. "We bonded over the flood in the basement. We worked like a team, like soulmates. It was wonderful. We revived our failing marriage. The Flood of '92 will forever live on in my memory."

"Not for me," said Twitch "There was no Flood of '92. She's been talking about this flood for the last year or two, and it never happened, Dr. Sack. I haven't minded so much, but now she's talking to the neighbors and folks at the coffee shop. No one remembers the Flood of '92 and being the mayor and all … why, it's getting a little embarrassing for me. Now, we had a little seepage in '95, but it was no flood. Maybe we did a little sweeping down there."

Twitch had been concerned enough about this situation to check out their town paper on microfiche at the state historical archives. In the spring of '92, *The Rivertown Weekly*, a thorough little rag, had covered the death of the town clerk's parrot and the new menu at the Chat 'n Chew, but it made no mention whatsoever of rising waters. Then he called the weather service where the records indicate that the snowfall

that winter had been moderate and that the spring temperatures were average—indication of a slow melt, both conditions
that counter-indicate flooding. Finally, he had decided to
check with George, the town plumber. Maybe a pipe had broken and over time Sally had reconfigured the incident into a
flood, he had reasoned. "George keeps pretty good records,"
Twitch said, "but he had no record of service at our house in
'92, although he came once in '95 to investigate the seepage
that I mentioned." He knew George knew why he was asking.
The agitated mayor became increasingly self-conscious about
his wife's peculiar memory, which he was now classifying as
a delusion.

Sack commended Twitch on his thorough investigation of
this matter. Sally said that she didn't need records and news-
papers to confirm or disconfirm her memories. They were
still her memories. And Sack, for whom longing is not just a
state, but a trait, knew just exactly what was going on with
Sally. They spoke to one another in language Twitch did not
quite understand, but he didn't mind. He let them talk and
did not complain about returning a few more times. "I long to
be closer to Twitch, but he's just too ... well, twitchy. He moves
around a lot. Look at him. Every inch of him is always busy.
And in the Flood of '92 he was busy with me." Sack did look at
him. Twitch's foot was kicking the air, his fingers fiddled with
the Kleenex box and he didn't just sit, he rocked. Confined to
a couch talking about a memory was clearly not this man's
preferred activity. Sack felt touched by the effort Twitch was
making.

"Well, as a problem, the Flood of '92 is irrelevant," Sack
finally said. (Our team had agreed about this from the start.)

And he told Sally to hang onto the memory—as if there were an alternative—because it was quite useful in giving the couple some direction. "Just get more Floods of '92 in your life, Sally," Sack said. Twitch didn't know what Sack was talking about, but Sally did.

END OF CASE

Sally continued to see Sack occasionally and, indeed, the memory didn't disappear, but it sized down considerably after the couple crafted a canoe together. None of us ever considered that Sally had been dissembling. No, this was clearly a memory, and Doppelmann especially appreciated that it was one imaginatively wrought, although for his taste, he said, somewhat short on drama.

Doppelmann, our resident expert on dissembling, inevitably would have the case of the dissembler to share with you, dear reader. And it would not be one of the tired tales of marital infidels or the charlatans of Vietnam or 9/11. But every bit an equal to sex and heroism, money offers an excellent opportunity for inspired lies.

Bunny and Roger

Roger suggested that he and Bunny consider marriage counseling when he became uneasy about the family finances. Both in their late thirties, they had been married for seven years. He was a successful accountant with a high-profile firm, but left the everyday family finances to Bunny who enthusiastically embraced the task. Modern, savvy people, they agreed that partners should understand equally the sometimes mysterious vicissitudes of the dollar. He left Bunny pretty much alone, even when the two did an extensive remodeling of their home which involved a renovated kitchen, the addition of two extra rooms, a new roof, chimney repair and landscaping. She had the opportunity to move thousands of dollars from one spot to another while Roger concentrated on his clients.

The couple first met at the home of friends who had decided that Roger needed the panache of a Bunny to keep him from suffocating in his gray flannel suit. Eye-catching and well-oiled, she charmed him right out of that suit. Roger told Doppelmann that he had been somewhat uneasy about Bunny from the start, a feeling he attributed to his poverty of experience with women. He had known little about her when they married, only that both of her parents died when she was in her early twenties and that she had dabbled, sometimes successfully, in a number of enterprises—hair styling, real estate, lipstick, designer clothing and power yoga.

Two weeks before their first visit with Doppelmann, Roger had had occasion to look at their overall financial picture and found several things that did not match up. The new roof had not cost $20,000 as Bunny reported, but $10,000, the landscaping not $15,000, but $8,000 and so on. Where, he asked Bunny, did the remainder go? First she said that he was apparently misreading the numbers, then that it must have gone to pay for the unforeseen extra expenses of the kitchen renovation. She attempted to cover herself at every point, but the whereabouts of money is, after all, Roger's area of expertise, and as such, he is trained to look for discrepancies, although he had been woefully heedless with regard to his own household budget. Even though he was still intimidated by his beguiling wife, she was not going to wiggle out of this; however, so far, she had successfully dodged the numbers.

Doppelmann was salivating. In case consultation, he painted mental pictures of the possibilities. "A woman like Bunny could be doing anything," he said. "Maybe she's in on an international scheme to replace original masterpieces with copies. Then she'll sell the originals on the black market. She's probably providing the trafficking costs of the smugglers and the compensation for the artists making copies. Or she could be investing in dog racing. That's it. She's bought herself some dogs … or maybe she's just going to Mystic Lake Casino. What a bore that would be."

"Doppelmann, give it up," said Regis-Rittenhouse.

She was right to intervene. Doppelmann needed our guidance on this case. He was not as intimidated by Bunny as Roger was, but he is a feverish fan of guile, cunning and trickery, a disposition seriously impairing his objectivity in this case. We warned him to avoid Bunny's clutches and agreed that one of the FABRCTR women should sit in on his next session to keep him on track and protect him from her wiles. I volunteered.

We met, and well, why Doppelmann and Roger couldn't handle this child, I do not know. Bunny was charming and nicely endowed, yes, but she was no bunny, she was a pussycat. Do big breasts actually blind these guys to seeing a person? Poor kid, she actually had to live with that endowment since she was twelve years old—I asked her. I also asked her if she had been diverting household funds for some personal enterprise.

She took her finger out of the dam. A personal history gushed forth that would compete favorably with the travails of Frank McCourt. The brief version is that her father left her mother when Bunny was five years old. Her mother was nearly destitute, so they lived in the projects for awhile. Mom had boy-friends whom Bunny never liked, but the first one agreed to pay the rent if they moved out of the projects. More rent-pay-ing boyfriends came along. When she was twelve, Bunny ran away because she hated her mother's current boyfriend more than any of the others. Mostly by hitchhiking, she managed to get herself from San Jose to St. Paul where she lived with an aunt for a few years. Then she began supporting herself, but never by selling her body, she said. With a flair for doing hair, she attended a styling school, and shortly after finishing, started her own salon. A few years later she sold it for a profit, invested money in other endeavors and increasingly socialized with quite chic, well-heeled people. She kept her background, of which she is profoundly ashamed, tightly concealed.

I watched the scales slip from the eyes of both Doppelmann and Roger as they reconfigured the woman in front of them, an orphan parading as a sophisticate.

"And where, honey, did you put all of that extra money?" I asked again.

"Habitat for Humanity."

"Habitat for Humanity?"

"Habitat for Humanity."

No one spoke for a minute or two. Roger may have been tallying his tax write-offs, but to give the man credit, he was more likely just recovering from shock.

"And I volunteer once a week." Nearly in unison, three of us furrowed our brows. "You know, pouring the foundation, hauling lumber, building the frame, gunning in screws, paint-ing. I like it."

Nearly in unison, three of us looked at her fingernails. Intact, clean, manicured. "I wear gloves," she said.

END OF CASE

Roger contacted Habitat for Humanity where Bunny's story was corroborated. He arranged for the tax write-off, and the two continued with Doppelmann for several months because some serious psychic realignment was in order. Bunny had created a persona that disappeared as quickly as last year's Halloween costume, although like that costume tucked in the back of the closet, she could always retrieve it. Roger would probably spend a long time deciding how to live with his unfrocked consort. Whatever he decides about that, our team had no problem deciding that Bunny has earned a place beside the owl, the orchid and the Artful Dodger.

Chapter V

QUIRKS AND COUNTER-QUIRKS

Throughout history nearly every tribe or village has had its misfit, eccentric, bohemian or outsider who was sometimes feared or ridiculed, maybe even driven away, but more frequently was just seen as an intriguing person who contributed to the local color and reminded others that the world is various and wondrous strange. A place for these people has continued even into modern times. Western movies, for example, have succeeded because of sidekicks, mavericks and drifters, characters with names like Hondo and Tonto and Pinto. We admire them for their gust and grit and remember them for being mysterious, possessed or wild-eyed.

Sadly, deviance from the norm has become undervalued and unappreciated in recent decades because the general public has become informed about psychology, a situation which unsettles the FABRCTR team.[5] Our colleagues across the land have contributed to this phenomenon by writing books and

---

[5]Especially Sack.

appearing as guests on talk shows. Some have brazenly begun their own shows, thereby exposing an unsuspecting public to the language of character predispositions and neuroses. Hardly anyone is ever just eccentric anymore; now a perfectly fine individual with an idiosyncracy is labeled with Rash-Impulse Syndrome, Idee Fixe Syndrome, Chronic Paleophobia, Premature Gag Reflex, Selective Listening Disorder and Dinner Party Paralysis (Mild, Moderate or Severe), terminology once exclusive to health care professionals. Meanwhile the public has forgotten that but for Idee Fixe Syndrome, *High Noon* would have no plot and but for Rash-Impulse Syndrome, we would have no westerns at all. The laity tosses these terms about like a handful of ill-begotten confetti.

And frequently they are tossed right into the face of a partner. Any marriage may now have its own misfit, maybe two. During skirmishes one partner, who may be feeling powerless, misunderstood or dismissed and who may also be harboring suspicions regarding her mate's mental and personality deficiencies, is likely to accuse him of Acute Listening Disorder, then escalate the conflict by yelping, "Chronic Listening Disorder." At risk of extinction is the simpler, time-honored and perfectly suitable epithet "jerk."

A typical example of the utility and hence the popularity of the label Chronic Listening Disorder (CLD) comes from the case of Maggie and Pete. Maggie had just returned from her evening commute home and was unleashing her frustration about freeway congestion and the rude guy in the red pick-up truck when she began to notice a glassy look in Pete's eyes. Already in a weakened condition, she became weaker still, but she did not fling herself on the floor, curl up in the fetal position and weep.[6] No, she hurled this accusation: "You are suffering from CLD. You need help." Clearly he would get none of it from Maggie. She also might have accused Pete of suffering from Dissociative State Caused by Fear of Intimacy, Type I, but using this cumbersome coinage is like trying to lob a head of cabbage over a net with a tennis racket. Chronic Listening Disorder is less cluttered, one of the reasons for its proliferation.

Second only to CLD in popularity among couples is the label Idee Fixe Syndrome (IFS). Persons with this disorder tend to preoccupy themselves with time, dirt or money and often feel driven to count things. Although we might pray for our brain surgeon or airplane mechanic to suffer from this disorder, most people do not find it particularly attractive in their partners. If an individual so afflicted does not have sufficient opportunity to edit footnotes, engrave cuff links or count coins at his job, he may have significant problems in his marriage. His partner, wearied of his behavior, may resort to the label IFS and in the heat of an argument this can quickly degenerate into "anal," which is more graphic but has lost its aura of erudition.

In a particularly severe case, Sack worked with a man who had night terrors due to his unshakable belief that micro-organisms were surfing in the folds of his sheets. His wife was convinced of his lunacy. Sack cooled her down and said to the man, "Well, of course they are, but they're surfing in the folds of your intestines too, so just make friends with them." A risk on Sack's part, this intervention could have gone badly, but it actually reduced the man's fears. In fact, it worked so well

---

[6]Hysteria is no longer vogue.

that he began giving names to his micro-organisms, a behavior that created further conflict with his wife who complained that he now spent all of his time on the Internet searching for names because, of course, he had to name every one. Sack told him that he should just pick names for his favorites.

In general Sack does well with IFS cases, but he made little headway with Fritz and Lizzie. Fritz contends that there is a right way and a wrong way to stack dishes in the dishwasher. He re-stacks Lizzie's stack, but because he often does this surreptitiously, she usually doesn't notice. One morning in her frustration to move along, she did notice: "*Stop reshuffling the dishes.* You're just like your mother. Both of you are just sick. You suffer from IFS and you both need meds." Because Fritz actually does suffer from Selective Listening Disorder (SLD), he had stopped hearing such remarks several years ago. Sack, who looks for a nice balance in a marriage, however it may be achieved, told the couple that Lizzie would probably just continue to erupt once in a while because she is Lizzie and meanwhile the SLD would successfully protect Fritz from her attacks.

Although many of these labels function as poison arrows, a few have lost their potency. Such is the case for Somewhat Annoying Melancholic Disorder, Type I (SAMD). While it is aptly named, definitely annoying and often disheartening, hardly anyone anymore is intimidated by the label. Comzac, a drug prescribed for this disorder, became so fashionable in the 80s that even unafflicted individuals said that they were afflicted just to keep up with their friends. Assuming a designer label appeal, the drug became psychiatry's own Calvin Klein. No matter how harsh a tone partners use, SAMD hardly wounds anyone anymore, not even when notched up to the more severe Highly Disruptive Melancholic Disorder, Type III. These labels are too likely to be misinterpreted as sympathetic or complimentary. Sack, who has suffered from both Type I and Type III, is pleased to see the stigma disappear.

Acute, Chronic and Idiosyncratic Mania fare even more poorly as marital missiles since the whole culture has turned manic. In fact, partners who are not sufficiently manic are sometimes perceived as passive or dull. Poets, who are generally read only in crisis situations, are infrequently manic, at least since Whitman or Ginsberg. If said with a slight snarl and sufficient disgust, maybe the label of mania could still inflict pain, but it no longer rises to the level of a disorder. Nevertheless, some less culturally astute partners will still resort to these terms.[7]

Quirks

Our team believes that it would behoove the modern partner to view her neurotic mate as a colorful eccentric, and for this we must shift the paradigm. Stop viewing his behavior as pathological and see it for what it is: a quirk. Infinitely resistant to extinction, a quirk is a benign behavior that appears unreasonable to everyone but the person behaving (see Glossary). It takes many forms and includes habits such as reading the entire contents of utility bill enclosures, changing TV channels by walking over to the set and eating only food that is white and smooth.

Although food, sleep and sex provide especially fine opportunities for quirks to flourish, hoarding and collecting

---

[7] None of this applies to children for whom mania, although a perfectly natural state for them, has a variety of labels.

behaviors compose the largest category of quirks. A good example is Lars of the Hulking Barn Case with his massive collection of farmstead cast-offs. (My husband Jake is another fine example. To save the marriage, he moved into the loft of our ample garage where he lives with his massive beetle, butterfly and grasshopper collections. We are both content as long as he comes regularly to the house for dinner, talk and an occasional romp between the sheets.) We have encountered collectors of African death masks, of toenail clippings, of loose screws. Sack knows the man who collects loose screws. This man says that the criterion for a screw to be selected for his collection is that he actually discovered it in a loosened condition and immediately removed it from its hole. He insists that he does not cheat, says Sack, that every screw in his collection was loose when he found it.[8]

While some quirks surface in early childhood, others form later. We don't know how they develop, but sometimes they seem like popcorn kernels just wallowing in the grease until they are hot enough to pop. Our team has spent some time speculating about the origins of a Regis-Rittenhouse quirk: It is the accumulation and assemblage of every letter, Post-it Note, laundry receipt, memo, chart, diagram, graph or missing person flyer to pass through her long, elegant fingers. Her office is filled floor-to-ceiling with files, drawers and boxes, each neatly labeled with date, contents and a fluorescent color-coded dot which, she tells us, is integral to her classification system. She hardly has room for her patients. If a couple brings along a child or in-law, one of the group is forced to sit on a box or a file, although no one seems to complain.

---

[8] This man may just *be* Sack.

She denies that her behavior is a quirk, says that it is simply effective information management and insists that we should all file missing person flyers and review them periodically because one of those persons is likely to show up at FABRCTR with a second wife. "I want to catch one of those bigamists red-handed," she says.

Some couples develop duplicate or co-ordinate quirks which can become bonding experiences for them. In fact, at FABRCTR we often recommend that they develop a shared quirk. For example, cross-dressing. A member of a couple who is not a cross-dresser can become disquieted and possibly envious if the other is, but the relationship becomes quite energized if they participate in this activity together. Especially if they don't tell anyone else. This enhances the intrigue because, even though the behavior is benign, it engenders a dirty-little-secret quality not unlike an extra-marital affair.

Doppelmann, in particular, endorses cross-dressing as a co-ordinate quirk. In fact, he enthusiastically described a couple who designate every Saturday night as dress-up night. Not only does the couple cross-dress, but they do so relative to a theme. On literary night, she may be Reverend Dimmesdale and he, Hester Prynne; on theater night, she Othello, he Desdemona; on history night, she Captain John Smith, he Pocahontas. (Doppelmann belabored all of this with extensive detail and never confessed that he was describing his own merry weekly caper with Nedra, whom I am having an increasingly difficult time envisioning at Copy Tech.)

Let's look at how this paradigm shift from pathologies to quirks would affect couples in conflict situations. First, Maggie and Pete: Instead of labeling Pete with a Chronic Listening

Disorder, she could just as well say to him, "Oh, there you go again, Pete, you little rascal, just fading into the ether." And Lizzie might say to Glen, "It's so endearing to me that you and your mother share this eccentric dishwasher thing." Such responses are likely to begin reshaping their inner spaces by calming everyone down, rekindling mutual fondness and possibly evoking nostalgia for western movies. Maybe they would inspire the couple to rent one that very night. Or they might be reminded of Milkie their cat who habitually snoozes on a pile of soiled laundry or attempts to nudge a shaft of sunlight across the floor. People are not annoyed by these quirks because they are exactly why their cats are valuable to them. And by the way, in their respective times both Whitman and Ginsberg were fine examples of quirky guys.

As I mentioned, we don't often know the origin of a quirk, although if we cannot find any evidence of eccentricity in the family tree, we might consider childhood swimming lessons, a schoolyard bully or a former marriage. A quirk cultivated in one marriage often transfers successfully to another as in one of Bloom's cases.

Lily, Gus and Herb

A volunteer at the local zoo, Lily's first husband Gus often brought home cast-offs. Orphans, he called them. He kept the racoons and wolves, suited to the northern climate, outside in cages and various other contraptions. But one, a binturong, native to Borneo and Malaysia, required warmer temperatures, so she stayed in their basement. He dubbed her Sweets in hopes of mollifying Lily who regularly used the basement on Mondays to do the family laundry. This binturong, with its shaggy brown coat, long white whiskers, generous ear tufts, deep chocolate eyes and carnivore teeth, was a playful creature with quite a gifted tail, one that could wrap around a human limb with a firm grip, all in play, of course. An arboreal creature, she generally hung out on the water pipes just above the laundry area. Whenever Lily came down with a load of wash, Sweets would leap off her perch, land on Lily's head and grab it with all five appendages. At 40 pounds, she nearly knocked the poor woman flat.

After a few of these experiences, Lily began trying a variety of tactics on laundry day. At first, she would bring down a banana, stand at the bottom of the stairs—away from Sweets' perch—and wait for her to fetch it. This worked for awhile, but Sweets, growing bored with the routine, only became more rambunctious. One day she did indeed knock her flat. Because Gus had told her that binturongs have a robust sweet tooth, Lily brought down some leftover Halloween candy the following Monday. After eagerly gnawing three Tootsie Pops down to their sticks, Sweets enjoyed a prize-winning sugar rush, which forced Lily out of the basement for an hour or two. After the rush passed, she returned with some grapes and a kiwi, but Sweets, apparently disappointed because she preferred the Tootsie Pops, expressed her feelings by urinating on poor Lily's head.

Laundry duty had become consistently hazardous, and Lily became distraught and bereft of ideas. There was no other place in their house for the washer and dryer and no other place for Sweets. Since she knew how much the binturong meant to Gus, she didn't want to disturb him with her travails. She might have asked him to do the laundry himself, but being Lily, she did not. She did, however, call her brother who helped her devise another solution; he offered her his bioterrorist suit. She really didn't know how he happened to own some of the things he owned, but she thought it unsecmly to ask and gratefully accepted the suit which, although somewhat ill-fitting, did protect her from most of Sweets' shenanigans. Every laundry day for years Lily wore this suit because binturongs live quite a long time in captivity, no zoo in the country would take Sweets and her brother didn't seem to need it anymore.

Eventually, Sweets expired as did Gus, a few months later. He had apparently picked up some virus at the zoo. The widowed Lily remarried. She and her new husband Herb moved into a house with first floor laundry facilities. No binturong resided in the basement or anywhere else on or near their property. Nevertheless, Lily continued to wear the bioterrorist suit on Mondays. At first Herb did not inquire about it. Apparently, he just didn't notice because he was rarely home on Mondays. After he retired, however, he couldn't help but see that she was knocking around in that ungainly suit on laundry day. When she wouldn't give it up at his request, he brought her to see Bloom who had worked with him and his first two wives. Lily explained her history with Sweets, and Bloom reminded Herb that harmless quirks in marriages are best tolerated whether you understand them or not.

END OF CASE

Our team is hopeful that this time around Herb might just catch on. Indeed, our normal neurotic couples have survived best in marriages where quirks are accepted or, better still, hospitably received like a cheerful neighbor bringing still another batch of crab apples. Together you and your neighbor might make your fifty-sixth jar of crab apple jam and be hanged what you do with them all. This leads us to one of FABRCTR's most innovative conceptualizations: the Counter-Quirk.

Counter-Quirks

A counter-quirk is a behavior either intrinsically present or developed over time that fits neatly into the quirk of a partner. Think tongue in groove (see Glossary). As a marriage ages, the peculiarities of couples, if not already present, are born of one another. The early stages of this dynamic are nearly imperceptible and often begin well before the couple is married or otherwise committed. Thus, it is nearly impossible to differentiate between a quirk and a counter-quirk. Don't even try.

Lily's quirk could easily be termed a counter-quirk as well because, after all, harboring a sub-tropical, arboreal mammal in a Minnesota basement is hardly prescriptive. Our team does not want to affront the memory of Gus by questioning his behavior, but we think you'll agree that it does qualify as quirky. And actually, if Herb is successful in overlooking Lily's bioterrorist suit every Monday, then their marriage becomes another fine demonstration of quirk/counter-quirk equilibrium.

Regis-Rittenhouse has been good enough to illuminate these concepts with her sketches of couple synchronization types:

Types of Couple
Quirk/Counter-Quirk Synchronization

Key: Q = Quirk   Q = Counter-Quirk | = Partner   (= Partner

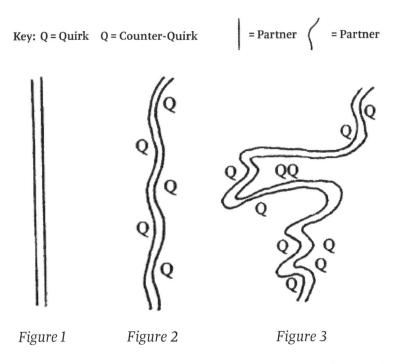

Figure 1   Figure 2   Figure 3

Figures 1, 2 and 3 are theoretical only because the quirks and counter-quirks are perfectly synchronized. These types do not exist in actuality, but if the quirkless partners of Figure 1 did exist, they would be lackluster and rarely invited to a soiree. Figure 2 represents a couple with modest quirks and Figure 3 a couple with very conspicuous quirks. The partners of the Figure 3 type would be particularly attractive to one another as well as to friends and likely invited to more soirees than they could possibly attend unless most of their quirks are of an introverted or mean-spirited nature.

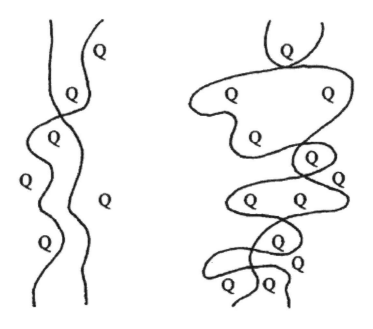

Figure 4   Figure 5

Figure 6

Figures 4, 5 and 6 represent actual couples. Figure 4 is the average couple. At times their quirks and counter-quirks are in loose harmony, but sometimes they get tangled up. These entanglements can lead to the pitiless labeling we discussed at the beginning of the chapter. Couples represented in Figure 5 are frequently out of sorts with one another. They are like a middle school orchestra concert for which rehearsals were scant and, as such, best avoided.

Figure 6 presents a theoretical paradox. One partner (wavy line) is extraordinarily quirky and the other (straight line) has no quirks whatsoever. Yet to live with a very quirky person without developing any counter-quirks is itself quirky. Therefore, perhaps that partner should not be represented with a straight line, but we couldn't think of another way to do it. Our team could not decide whether this type of couple is very fragile or very stable or whether it should even be included in our study. Then Bloom made the case that the marriage of Lily and Herb may represent just such a couple and that further examination of their marriage may lead to a clearer vision of this type. "Never," said Doppelmann, "there's no logic to it, no logic to be found. We're all like Alice trying to make sense of Wonderland."

Sense or nonsense aside, Doppelmann and the rest of our team believes that we have sensible advice for the reader. We request that you seriously consider the value of our new paradigm and its superiority over the old one which encourages people to paste labels on their partners as routinely as Chiquita pastes stickers on bananas. We have nothing against a spirited fight and even Sack, who knows better than any of us the humiliation of an epithet cast one's way by a copiously informed partner, believes that a good one can be entertaining. Perhaps you will consider us naive utopians for suggesting that tolerance for the household misfit can be achieved by shifting the lens, but even Regis-Rittenhouse, who would give up her files before submitting to the label of naive utopian or any other kind of utopian, joins us—somewhat short of begrudgingly—in our request.

Chapter VI

SOVEREIGNTY, SPACE AND AN OCCASIONAL NAP

A contemporary issue for married men is the quest for sovereignty. Early on man hunted beasts and speared fish. For millenniums it went like this. Men resourcefully headed into the forests, hills, plains or mountains, then returned home with salmon, quail or wapiti. Meanwhile, women wove baskets, gathered roots and burped their babies. Everyone was satisfied so no one had to sit around and talk about it. As time passed appreciation for the captured quarry faded. These animals were deemed messy, their carcasses had to be cleaned, carved up and stored, and freezer space was limited, especially for the wapiti. Besides that, man was out stalking and killing innocent wildlife when he should have been home bagging leaves for the compost pile. Hunting, and yes, even fishing, became undervalued in society as a whole as well as a source of contention within the marriage. And with them went male sovereignty. Man wondered, What do I have that is my own?

In recent decades women have asked the same question. First, there was just a lot of talk, and then a remarkable thing happened. Women began going on wilderness excursions, not just metaphorical or virtual journeys, but actual forays into the woods and mountains. Men became confused and mistrustful. Exactly what were these women up to? They shouldered canoes over rocky portages and carried 40-pound backpacks up steep mountain trails, or at least they said they did. They contrived these journeys in small covens and during the planning stages could sometimes be overheard in telephone conversations in which they were making decisions about reading material for the trips. They were not taking along Harlequin romances—harmless enough—not even Jane Austen, Iris Murdoch or Barbara Kingsolver novels. No, they were taking books of meditations, poetry and *chants*. These behaviors intimated the shadowy, the sinister, the unknown. Women, of course, have always been mysterious to men, and sometimes even untrustworthy, but this was more baffling than anything these men had encountered in their time. Whatever were they doing in the woods?

Women were finding sovereignty in the woods. And while they have been doing that, men have been developing a growing desire to be more sovereign within their own homes. Sovereignty is the dominion over one's own person in space and time, especially with regard to eating, drinking and naps (see Glossary). A recent survey indicated that men have no sovereignty whatsoever in about 80% of homes with couples. And the other 20% are either households where gay men reside or where the female partner is intrinsically unorthodox and preoccupied with literature, film or dance. These disturbing statistics may be changing. Many men are beginning to demand their own rights to the refrigerator and the kitchen sink as well. This does not necessarily mean that they want to clean the refrigerator or the sink, although 27% of men say that they do. (This, by coincidence, is the same percentage of men who prefers to keep their remote control attached to their belts rather than placed on a table near the TV set, a more democratic location, although it is unlikely that it is the same 27%. For men in homes with many remote control items, such as four TV sets, two VCRs and three automatic garage doors, this can become quite cumbersome.)

Gaining sovereignty in the household for men has been no easy task. In addition to what appears to be an inherent awkwardness with it, men often fail to convey sufficient motivation. Both Doppelmann and Sack, however, say that they have encountered a scattering of men who do. Further research on this issue is in order, especially as it relates to Domestic Denial which refers to the tendency of one partner to believe that he has actually done more than his fair share of the household tasks (see Glossary). This is more prevalent in men than in women, but given that it has also been found in lesbian households, experts suspect that members of both genders have the capacity to harbor the fiction.

Whether she has scaled vertical precipices, orchestrated a lawsuit against the Vatican, raised award-winning malamutes, managed fifty apartment units or settled for a life with the soaps, a woman cannot shake her propensity to govern the household, although this may be subtle and not immediately apparent to outsiders. If the couple has a woman, she likely presides over the carpool, chili powder, philodendrons, vinegar, bleach, stray buttons, pencil sharpener and family calendar, especially the family calendar. With such a broad and diverse sphere of influence, she is perpetually at risk of encroaching upon her partner's sovereignty. (It was because I had been encroaching so flagrantly on Jake's sovereignty—well, at least he thought so—that he moved with all of his little dead creatures to the garage.)

To explore this issue in greater depth, we reviewed our cases and agreed that Bloom had the one most germane to the issue of male sovereignty. Our team hopes that you appreciate the great courage she demonstrates in sharing this case for she has exposed her own vulnerability, indiscretion and, well, blunder.

Griff and Charity

This couple had been married for 38 years when they began couple counseling with Bloom. Griff is a large, lumpy, affable and intellectually unburdened man. In the early part of the marriage he had engaged in tavern camaraderie and heavy drinking, but has long since settled down. Charity is a comely, slightly plump woman with short hennaed hair and shrill gold earrings—several pairs, according to Bloom. She has a smile that reaches a sorry peak about the same time that her discomfiture does. The couple has three grown children and four grandchildren. Bloom thinks that, in general, the marriage flourishes on low expectations.

Griff wandered out of the marriage counseling after the first few visits, perhaps, Bloom surmised, because it did not quite resonate with him. This left Bloom and Charity to themselves. At about this point, Charity's agitation about her marriage shifted from moderate to severe and laser-beamed its way straight into Griff's midsection. She watched over that midsection as scrupulously as a mother attending to her child's growing tendency to scratch herself in her privates. While her anxiety grew to a fevered pitch during her meetings with Bloom, she vowed that she was exercising patience and discretion when she was with Griff alone. Bloom doubted this and I suspect that at this point she furrowed her brow ever so slightly, but Charity would not have noticed.

If Griff's midsection was Charity's theme song, her Chocolate Desire brownies were its refrain. After she had made the weekly batch for her grandchildren's visits, she kept a close and accurate count because Griff had a habit of depleting the supply. Bloom encouraged Charity to focus on interests of her own—to call friends, to join a 12-step group or to take her grandchildren to the science museum—and was heartened by her surprisingly vigorous response. She joined a water aerobics class, read to the blind and organized a Bible study group for women at her church. And after these things were up and running, she returned boomerang-style to brownie enumeration.

This failure only intensified Bloom's determination. She helped Charity to explore her past more deeply. Perhaps, she suggested, Charity had never learned to attend to her own need because, as the oldest of seven children, she learned to focus only on the needs of others. Charity became quite engaged in this pursuit and even brought in two of her sisters to talk about the family dynamics. She read books, not only the usual riffs on birth order, male depression and compulsive eating, but even *Women Who Run With the Wolves*—although she didn't much like it. Still Charity persisted in focusing on Griff's expanding belly. "I measured it while he was sleeping," she confessed one day with her big, uncomfortable smile. Bloom tried to follow Charity's narrative, she told us, but she became distracted by her own attempt to envision the contortions necessary to measure Griff's waistline while he was sleeping. Surely it would involve rolling that fleshy man over. Wouldn't he awaken? Perhaps he is an especially sound sleeper, she thought, and Charity might be quite strong. As much as she wanted to know the details, she did not inquire further because she reminded herself it is not professional to ask clients questions out of sheer curiosity. The rest of us wanted to know too, but with Bloom at risk of losing her grip on the case, she needed our focused guidance.

The following week the saga continued. Charity pleaded with Bloom, "What can I do about the brownies? I put them in the basement freezer where he would not think to look and if he did, I couldn't imagine he would actually eat frozen brownies. He found them within hours ... minutes, fished them out and ate them without even using the microwave!" The belly-brownie watch was her project, her *raison d'etre.* Charity wept. Bloom lamented the dear woman's helplessness, as well as her own. Nothing she said could make a difference for Charity; her words had fared about as well as noses on ancient Egyptian statues.

Working with this docile recalcitrant, Bloom became increasingly distraught herself. So far, she had engaged in a futile campaign to drag the woman to higher ground. The next time she consulted with our team, Sack said that Charity suffers from Acute Perseverence Disorder, Regis-Rittenhouse said it is Distaff Care-taking Syndrome and Bloom, in a fit of self-reproach, diagnosed herself with Acute Imposter Syndrome. She had become convinced that she was a failure as a marriage counselor. She joined a health club, lifted weights and started tai chi classes. She attended seminars on personality disorders and compulsive behavior, read books on counter-interference (see Glossary) and started drinking microbrewed beer—although never while she was working. Still Charity came week after week.

The weekly ritual upended, however, the day that Charity arrived for her session so distraught that Bloom became convinced a crushing geologic disaster had destroyed the city. No such event had occurred. Charity gathered herself together enough to blurt out this news: "Griff is wearing his belt a notch further out."

The case was an unmitigated failure. In an instant, Bloom's professional life flashed before her. Her graduate advisor had praised her master's thesis on the dynamics of the nicotine-free, shame-based, dual-career, childless couple. When the country's leading expert on marital strife was in town, he chose her, Rose Ellen Bloom, to be on the panel of local experts and to lead one of his workshops. And she is a founding partner of the highly regarded FABRCTR where she had successfully worked for fifteen years. These achievements rose like rainbow bubbles into the air, collided, then dissolved. Her mind went blank and then she watched herself as she screeched, "Griff's brownie consumption and waistline are none of your freaking business. Leave him alone!" After she and Charity stared at one another for an indeterminate period of time, Charity blinked her eyes and said that maybe she was finished for today.

Bloom was overwrought about her uncharacteristically unprofessional behavior, although relieved that she had said freaking instead of that other f-word. She wondered if she harbored a deep-seated, unresolved issue or if this was the harbinger of another midlife crisis. With shame and remorse

Bloom consulted her own therapist and related the incident. She got a puzzling response. At first she thought that Dr. St. John was having a seizure. Bloom was about to dial 911 on her cell phone when she realized that the woman had merely burst into a frenzy of laughter. She recovered shortly and although Bloom was quite perplexed, she felt much better. Later she speculated that Dr. St. John might have lost her bearings with a client once or twice herself. Whether true or not, the idea was comforting.

Charity called Bloom a few months later to thank her for her help. She said she was not coming to counseling for now because things were actually going quite well between Griff and herself. She had stopped baking brownies altogether, but regularly took her grandchildren out for ice cream.

END OF CASE

After Bloom's initial relief that Charity was doing well and would be unlikely to report her to the Board of Marriage Therapists for unprofessional behavior, she became bewildered. She could not recall that unbridled behavior had been mentioned as an effective counseling technique in her training, no matter how successful it seemed to have been in this case. We told her not to worry about it. Maybe a Baskin-Robbins had opened up in Charity's neighborhood, maybe her grandchildren said they were sick and tired of her brownies or maybe she got better advice from Dr. Phil. "After all, we encounter mysteries even physicists cannot explain," Sack said.

Exercising characteristic evenhandedness, our team wants to emphasize that a male partner is just as likely to encroach upon his partner's sovereignty regarding food and weight matters as a female partner. In fact, we have frequently encountered a type who will become fixated on a little extra flesh his wife has collected while oblivious to the extra flesh under his own belt. Inspired by Charity's gumption and recognizing a man's need for humility—if not humiliation, Regis-Rittenhouse developed a technique to deal with this type: She sizes him up and just as he begins to complain about his wife's weight—she can see it coming—she pops up from her chair, pulls a tape measure out of a file and measures his waistline in real time. These men rarely return to FABRCTR, but their wives often call to tell Regis-Rittenhouse that for a month or two their husbands had refrained from making cryptic, weight-related remarks and to request that she come to their homes with her tape measure. Like a flu shot, her intervention has no permanency; nevertheless, she refuses the requests: "One hit, that's all they get."

Sack, who has increased the size of the roll under his belt since Shirley left, has little interest in the food related issues of sovereignty. He considers the most serious encroachment upon sovereignty, and particularly upon male sovereignty, to be tinkering with naps. He claims that he and Hobbes never interfere with one another's naps and that this is exactly as it should be between two humans. The rest of the team feels somewhat less passionately about this, but we do agree that beyond the ages of four or five, it does seem reasonable that a person should have authority over his or her own naps whenever and wherever they occur. However, we would soon discover that the whole realm of napping within a marriage can be quite intricate. Probably due to Sack's passion for the issue, he was chagrined when it was Regis-Rittenhouse who introduced a case highly apropos for our study. He did not believe that she had the requisite devotion and feared that she might toss off the nap as a mere psychological bauble. As far as any of us knew, she never even took naps and, in fact, the idea strained our collective imaginations. But Sack could not dispute that the following nap case is a ten.

Buzzie and Lou Ann

Buzzie and Lou Ann, a middle-aged couple, had been married for only five years when they began seeing Regis-Rittenhouse. She helped them to resolve a variety of minor problems, like who should rake the yard—they hired a neighbor—and when to make the bed—they decided on Mondays. After these and other successes, they would return to a seemingly intractable problem: Naps, specifically Buzzie's naps. He could catch a few nods anywhere, just drop his head and be gone. "My method of nap-taking saves time," he said. "Any pause in the action and I'll make good use of it. That's how I avoid boredom and stay invigorated." When his long-winded uncle calls him, Buzzie greets him, closes his eyes, sets his internal timer for five or ten minutes and his brain on theta waves, wakes up long enough to say, "Yeah, un-huh," repeats the process until his uncle runs out of steam and awakens just in time to say, "Great talking to you again, Uncle B. J."

Even Regis-Rittenhouse was impressed with his ingenuity and proficiency. Unfortunately, the benefits of his aptitude for napping, a gift he clearly prizes, were entirely lost on Lou Ann. She didn't mind what he did with Uncle B. J., but besides the Saturday afternoon chore-avoiding naps, it was the church, movie, concert and golfing naps that nettled her. The church problem, however, was actually now benefitting Lou Ann because Buzzie had only agreed to come to FABRCTR because it is housed in a former church building. He has developed an affinity for churches because he has experienced some of his most delicious naps in their pews; however, he did not have any delicious naps with Regis-Rittenhouse around. She was a stickler and rang a cowbell with the slightest indication that he might be nodding off.

"It's an embarrassment for me," said Lou Ann. "We have a good friend who plays French horn in the orchestra. He sits in the back on a raised platform with the other horn players and looks straight out across the audience. From there Ivan can see Buzzie's head bobbing down until his pate is aimed directly at him. His best friend … playing his heart out and Buzzie is snoozing."

"And that's when she punches me in the arm," said Buzzie.

"You snore during the hushed, melodic parts."

"I don't snore, I purr, and no one but you can hear it."

"And on the golf course … you never even see my last two or three shots. That two or three could be five or six shots, ha, for all you know."

Lou Ann was working herself into shrill. She glared at Regis-Rittenhouse and fulminated, "How does he even do it? He's nodding off in the f**king golf cart."

After Regis-Rittenhouse helped her cool down, she suggested that the logical consequences (see Glossary) of his habitual naps would eventually be punishing enough for Buzzie to give them up on his own and that Lou Ann would do well to back off. "But he never has any consequences. Nothing ever gets the best of him when he naps. If only that would happen, but it never does. Ivan doesn't even mind." Regis-Rittenhouse assured her that the time would come.

Well, it almost did. One weekend while visiting the Field Museum in Chicago, the two were planning their last 20 minutes before the museum closed. Lou Ann wanted to stay longer at the African exhibit and Buzzie decided to check out the Eskimos. They agreed to meet at the five o'clock closing time in the center hall near Sue the Tyrannosaurus rex. When she arrived at the appointed time, he was seriously missing. She circled Sue carefully looking for Buzzie who often develops a chameleon-like quality while napping. As she was checking underneath the hulking vertebrate, the guard spotted her, announced closing time, then unceremoniously escorted her out. She protested, "But my husband is in here somewhere." The guard apparently considered her protestations a ruse devised by some crazy broad who wanted to swipe a dinosaur digit. She was about to raise both volume and intensity when she remembered: Logical consequences ... logical consequences. He'll spend the night in this cavernous place, be starved by morning and then be forever cured of his indiscriminate napping, she thought. She returned to their hotel, enjoyed a lovely dinner, then fell soundly asleep on the clean white sheets of a great big bed. Revenge, ah, sweet revenge.

While she was having breakfast in the hotel restaurant the next morning, Buzzie sauntered in, none the worse for wear. This was her first deflation. Then he described his odyssey: He awakened in an igloo shortly after closing time, realized that he had been locked in and decided to continue his nap. Sometime after midnight he was discovered by a night watchman who shared a sandwich with him and said that as long as it was so late, he could just sleep on one of the cots in a back room. He awoke quite early in the morning, wandered around and discovered vending machines in a darkened lunch room where he acquired a bag of peanuts and a Coke. Sitting at a picnic table apparently sized for schoolchildren, he ate his snack, then put his head down for a final wink. "And now I feel great," he said to Lou Ann.

On Monday Lou Ann called Regis-Rittenhouse. "Logical consequences do not exist for this man. He's bewitched or something. What can I do?" Lou Ann was heating up again and also losing heart. When the couple came to see her the next day, Regis-Rittenhouse tried an alternative route: "You know, Buzzie, you're no spring chicken." (True. He was nearly 50.) She continued, "Maybe you have a touch of narcolepsy. Have you considered checking out the Sleep Disorders Center?" Lou Ann was heartened by this suggestion, but Buzzie clearly considered it an assault on his pride and, yes, on his identity. "This is like asking Tiger Woods to see a physician because his golf scores are so consistently and unrealistically low," he said.

Buzzie, however, capitulated to the will of the women, followed through at the clinic and emerged untarnished. When he told Lou Ann that his attending physician pronounced him neurologically sound and "a damn good sleeper," Lou Ann's anger disintegrated into hopelessness. "Better single than this. I can do single, but I can't do this. I have married a man who just keeps checking out on me. He goes into this space that is all his own," she said. Regis-Rittenhouse reassured her, "There are other avenues to explore."

She put Lou Ann through the usual paces. To buy a little time and distract her from her obsession with Buzzie's naps, they explored Lou Ann's family history. Like nearly everyone else, Lou Ann enjoys talking about herself. Had her father neglected her? Abandoned her? She calmed down. No, he had taken her along with her older brother Lonnie and little sister Liza to the movies every Saturday, and he had attended most of her swim meets. No, as far as she knew, he had not napped during either the movies or the swim meets. "And the whole family went camping. My parents were fine. They did have their differences and finally divorced when I was in college, but they are still friendly with each other, and we all get together for holidays."

"But what about naps? Do you remember anything about naps?"

"Sure, when I was little, I had to take naps. Oh ... but, you know what, my parents took naps. They took naps every Sunday afternoon."

"Did they?"

"Yes, and it was weird. I didn't think so at the time. They had twin beds in their bedroom, but that wasn't where they took naps. They climbed up into the attic where we stored our camping equipment. Then they would pull up the ladder and shut the trap door. We kids just went about our business and didn't think too much about it; that's just what they did. Parents are strange, we all knew that. Sometimes Lonnie would hang around below the trap door with one of those horn things that amplifies sound. Then one day, while they were napping and my little sister was playing with her Barbies—I was around 13, maybe 14—Lonnie took me aside and whispered in my ear that Mom and Dad were having sex up there. At first this was exciting, intriguing, kind of exhilarating for me ... well, you know, by then I had an active hormone or two myself. A few weeks after Lonnie told me I was at a slumber party and told my seven best friends about it. We giggled the rest of the night thinking about two old people up there tossing around on a sleeping bag and getting it on. My sister Liza—we eventually told her—says they're still up to it. Imagine, divorced, practically 70 years old, and they still get together for an occasional 'nap' in the attic."

"Maybe you and Buzzie could take naps like that," Regis-Rittenhouse offered.

And they did.

And they do. They don't have an attic, but they put a queen-sized mattress in their ample, windowless storeroom where they light a half dozen ylang ylang-mimosa scented candles when they visit it every Sunday afternoon. Buzzie stays awake for the sex and then they both nod off.

END OF CASE

Doppelmann does not think that a storeroom has the mystique of an attic, but Sack was roundly thrilled with the results: "And it will only get better. The more Lou Ann matures, the more she'll come into her own with naps. Give her a few years and she'll join him in the golf cart too." Lou Ann's attitude toward naps had softened; in fact, at the end of treatment, they had taken on a charmed, almost metaphysical quality for her.

Bloom redirected us into a discussion of the implications of the case before we could stop her. "Certain schools of thought would find Regis-Rittenhouse brilliant in pairing the positive reinforcers of love-making, ritual and fellowship with the punishing aspects of Buzzie's naps." We noted that the reverse, of course, is that the naps would forever contaminate the love-making, ritual and fellowship, thereby thwarting any hope for the couple. Our courageous Regis-Rittenhouse, never risk-averse, had a successful case.

Bloom also pointed out that another school of thought might generate more elaborate interpretations of the whole business, especially of Lou Ann's family history, but the rest of us finessed further analysis. After all, the whole matter was settled. The right conditions had occurred for one partner to maintain sovereignty over his naps without undue interference from his mate. We were satisfied.

Chapter VII

HEROES, MAIDENS AND ROMANCE

A proper romance has always required a hero, a maiden and a dragon. But neither the hero nor the maiden prospers in modern times, a condition which raises questions about the unremittingly robust popularity of romantic fantasies and expectations. Some modern men have tried diligently to be heroes in their marriages, but with limited success. Sack thinks that the standards are too high and should be lowered a notch or two. The rest of our team disagrees: This problem is too convoluted to be fixed by merely cooking the books.

Because the traditional story requires that the hero kill the dragon to free the maiden, the hero depends upon the existence of both maidens and dragons, not to mention public acceptance of dragon-slaying as a sport. None of this augers well for the modern hero. For one thing, dragons are nearly extinct. Maidens, then, have less to fear, therefore less dependence on heroes. And some have become so bold and fit, they would probably slay their own dragons if there were enough to slay. The true maiden has become very rare. And while an occasional man will still select one for a wife, he is likely to change his mind before long and tell her to grow up and find a job.

The Hero

Our team began our exploration of this topic with a brief review of the history of heroes. While it seems as though there may have been heroes at some time in the past, perhaps during Paleolithic times, the evidence is inconclusive. The remains, for example, of a Cro-Magnon man found buried in ice on a mountaintop only confirm that he got there one way or another, not necessarily for heroic purposes. Perhaps he was searching for food merely for himself with no intention whatsoever of sharing. We don't know.

The Ancient Greeks were particularly caught up in the heroic ideal. Although little is known about their maidens, many had wives. Odysseus had the faithful Penelope. While she knitted and unknitted, he journeyed about engaging in tasks, most of which were as grisly and hazardous as dragon-slaying. He was gone, however, for twenty years and these days women either do not want their husbands to be gone for that long or else to be gone for good. Besides, only a few wives are still handy at knitting.

War and revolution have generated heroes. We know who they are because we find them bronzed up and astride horses in the middle of village greens. But these are just regional or national heroes. General Sherman, for example, may have been a hero in the northern United States, but we do not find him on a pedestal in Atlanta. Simon Bolivar is not memorialized in Toronto, Napoleon in Greenland or Ataturk in Montana. Even status as a public hero, however, may do nothing for heroic credibility in one's own home. No substantial evidence exists that Abraham Lincoln or Audie Murphy, national heroes, were considered so by their respective wives. For all we know, Mrs. Lincoln and Mrs. Murphy may have said, "But what exactly have you done for *me* lately?" If heroes are just geographical phenomena or temporary heroes like Mussolini or Hitler, what can we expect in our own households? "Maybe some guy who helps rake the leaves," says Regis-Rittenhouse, "if we're lucky."

In considering more recent times—well, times in which some of us were actually alive—we rely on Sack, the member of our team who is always willing to conjure up his own past. He says that men in the 1950s were heroes if they owned a motorcycle or a car with pin-striping and in the sixties if they wore beads or skipped classes to protest something.

"Adolescent envy and insecurity, Sack," said Regis-Rittenouse. "You just wanted to be more like your more adventurous, committed or prosperous peers."

"But I'm sure before we're finished with our exploration of heroes, Howie, that your memories of those decades will shed light on the concept," said Bloom

Doppelmann, who had recently enrolled in a fencing class, was particularly animated about the whole issue. He said that deep inside of every man is a hero who longs for nobility, honor, strength, valor and, above all, the desire to be a great protector and lover. "The hero is a man in charge of his own destiny," he proclaimed and then went on at some length.

Regis-Rittenhouse called his riff indulgent fantasy. "What a concept. The hero rescues the maiden, marries her, then remains infinitely wise, articulate, prosperous and sexy," she said. "No one like that exists. And who would want it? Sometimes we just need somebody to pick on." Bloom winced. (And Doppelmann told us later that the Regis-Rittenhouse relationship with whomever was not going well.)

The mythical hero's journey conjures up forces of darkness, danger and intrigue, but the modern man's journey often consists of walking from the TV set to the refrigerator. A hero needs a situation advantageous for hero-making, and marriage just does not seem to be that situation. At this point our team might have agreed that heroism may be an irrelevant issue for us to explore since its relationship to marriage may be negligible, except for this: Wives, who in spite of overwhelming evidence to the contrary, keep waiting for their husbands to be heroes like groupies waiting at the wrong stage door. Of those who have visited our counseling center, 87% have confided in us that they are quite disappointed that their husbands are not heroes. (Fewer than 5% of men are disappointed that their wives are not heroes.) Of gays and lesbians, only 55% are disappointed that their partners are not heroes.[9] Mothers of sons, of course, hope that their male offspring might be more effective heroes than their fathers, and some are buying them gender-free toys to increase that probability.

Due to the magnitude of the disappointment we discovered, especially among straight people, we agreed to look more closely at specifics. We designed a questionnaire in which we asked each female partner to complete this sentence:

My partner would be a hero if he would _____.

Here are some typical responses:

---

[9]Further study is in order.

> -rub my back
> -wash my back
> -scratch my back
> -mutate into Ralph Fiennes
> -rise to the occasion

Some wives noted in parentheses that they did not want their husbands to be heroes at all, that they would rather have a homespun man who did not attract the attention of other females. Amy, for example, had been married to a local rock musician whom she turned in for a post office clerk.

"A withering, pathetic, insipid grasp of the hero concept," Doppelmann sputtered when he saw the results. "Where are the forces of darkness? Where are the perils? Where is the sacrifice? Where is the split second victory?"

"At the movies," I said.

Doppelmann was as entangled in this project as Benjamin with Mrs. Robinson and his behavior equally unstable. We waited for him to settle down and then agreed that our research was incomplete unless we asked the husbands and partners what they thought. We gave them this sentence to complete:

My partner would consider me a hero if I _____.

Here are some typical responses:

> -quit my job at OfficeMax and became a successful disc jockey
> -saved an entire family from a burning building—assuming that the media picked up on it
> -mutated into Bruce Willis

A scattering of these responses came within reach of the hero concept, so Doppelmann was somewhat appeased, although still they did not quite rise to his expectations: "No one mentioned dragons at all and only a handful mentioned muggers and thieves, the capture of which can at least tweak the romantic imagination," he said. "Great orators and champions of the poor are lost on this crowd." He began to lose interest.

Maidens and Romance

Bloom suggested that a discussion of maidens could shed light on the hero concept. No one could agree, however, on what a maiden actually is. She seemed curious and touching and quaint to us, like crocheted doilies on the armrests of a grandmother's chair. We needed a description or definition of some kind. Regis-Rittenhouse described the maiden as helpless, fragile and coy—therefore untrustworthy. Doppelmann would have none of it. "Victoria," he said, "your unfavorable description suggests that you have an ego defense of a long-held, deeply-imbedded, but unconscious yearning to actually *be* a maiden."

"Not one bloody ounce of me wants to be a maiden, Doppelmann," said Regis-Rittenhouse.

Bloom joined the fray and defended the maidens: "I think you're failing to see the clever, witty and adventuresome features of the world's maidens, Victoria. What about Princess Leia? She was wily and courageous."

"Nonsense. A few braids wrapped around a woman's ears aren't enough to qualify her as a maiden," said Regis-Rittenhouse.

About all we could agree on was that the stereotypical qualities of the maiden are no longer widely admired, and then we questioned whether they ever were. By the time Sack brought up Darwin, we had all settled down. "He noticed a natural coyness in females of many species," Sack said, "so it must have had some survival value. Maybe, though, if Darwin were doing his research now, he would find more female iguanas with brazen libido."

Coyness may have been chic on the Galapagos during Victorian times, but not here and now. Many women have contributed to its demise by becoming athletic and self-sufficient. Abandoning the sidelines to kick, catch, coach and critique, a few have come suspiciously close to being heroes themselves. So if women are not coy maidens and men are not heroes, what happens to romance? And what is romance?

Well, it's a love affair, which, as you probably know from experience, is quite brief. And it thrives on pursuit. On the face of it, males are the pursuers. And they cannot help it, so we shouldn't ridicule them for it. They are merely doing what their counterparts in the animal world—the buffalo, the mallard, the katydid and the mollusks—do. In fact, we need to give them some help with it. They need it because, unlike lizards, they do not have an inflatable throat sack that turns bright colors to dazzle the female during the mating season. Neither do they have the mandible of beetles, the horns of stags or the canines of chimpanzees to fight off competitors. It is true that at one point in history males fought duels, but this is currently regarded as unseemly.[10] Man must find alternative ways of charming and impressing the female. Sack again

_____

[10]Doppelmann is disappointed about this.

reminded us of the pin-striping that was done in the fifties and suggested that tattoos and body piercing are its current equivalents. "Only in some segments of society," said Bloom.

While romance thrives on pursuit, pursuit thrives on intrigue, secrecy, obstacles, adventures, delays, near-death experiences, and above all, actual death experiences, which freeze the romance for eternity. This, of course, brings to mind Romeo and Juliet, whose families harbored antipathy for one another. Our team became intrigued with an alternative ending to this tale. If they had survived, with which family would they have spent Thanksgiving? When Bloom reminded us that Thanksgiving was not celebrated in sixteenth-century Verona, we thought she was being too literal and just picking at details. However they might have struggled with their holiday and family visitation schedule, they would eventually lose interest in the romance and explore other activities, we concluded.

Romance is like deep sea diving: exhilarating, enchanting, resplendent and surreal, but eventually airless. Without more oxygen, the end result is suffocation. Besides, people in love can't think straight. The pleasure zones of the brain activate while memory and attention zones inactivate. Long term this makes romance impractical because jobs would be lost, cars dented, dental appointments forgotten, beer and milk spilled. Fortunately, romance and sex are not the same thing, but some couples are confused about this. As they mature, they usually figure it out and are relieved.

The hero-maiden-romance triad came into greater focus for our team after Sack began his case with Sophie. This is the story of a woman twice obsessed with romance, then woefully disheartened by it. The team was uncertain whether Sack was the best choice to do the counseling because of his current vulnerability, but since nearly all of our cases involve matters of love and loss, and since this one involved a particularly fair maiden—well, not technically a maiden—we agreed that it might distract Sack from his current chagrin. Doppelmann, who was undergoing emergency gall bladder surgery, was not around for this decision and later came to rue those stones for more than one reason. After his first peek at Sophie in the waiting room, he described her as an ethereal being with the lunar beauty of the maidens depicted by Titian and Raphael.

Sophie, Cassidy and Charles

Sophie, 35 years old, has had two marriages, the first ending in divorce, the second in annulment. She worked as a librarian in a small branch of the city library system.

In her first meeting with Sack, she was awash in self-doubt. "What I thought I wanted wasn't what I wanted, but I thought it was what I needed and it wasn't what I needed either, but now I know that I am desperately in need of some help," she began. "I'm questioning whether being married to an actual person is reasonable for me. My husbands were both wrong for me and they seemed so right at the time. They were just less, much less, than I thought they would be or maybe ... maybe they were just too much for me. I don't know."

Sophie's first marriage had been to Cassidy, a professional wrestler. Ah, thought Sack, a contemporary version of the dragon slayer. That association needed some adjustment when Sophie revealed his stage name, Cass the Bad Ass. As his memory issued a configuration of Cassidy, a low gray cloud gradually enveloped Sack. The wrestling channel, ah yes, that brute ... and with this celestial spirit, he thought. What cynical god had created that unfortunate match?

When it all began, Sophie had been mindlessly surfing with the remote and paused at the wrestling channel. In the weeks to follow, she took a voyeuristic peek every now and then when her roommates Lydia and Ruth were otherwise engaged. The three of them were active members of a conservative Protestant sect and unlikely to indulge themselves in entertainment which skirts the edges of propriety and virtue. Sophie, however, was intrigued and increasingly found herself in front of the TV or at her desk exploring *www.prowrestling.org.*

But it was when Sophie first glimpsed Cassidy's large, raw, powerful body lunging at another large, raw, powerful body that an electrical charge surged through her—from torso to limbs to fingertips—and ignited an obsession. Her double life began. First, she just kept track of Cassidy's matches and attempted to dispatch her roommates by suggesting errands and entertainment options for them. They grew suspicious, asked too many questions and kept an increasingly closer watch on her. She had to think of something else, so she told Ruth and Lydia that she had taken a second job working evenings at Sportsall where she took stock inventory. She was actually spending the time at a sports bar that aired Cass-the-Bad-Ass matches to the delight of a scattering of his enthusiastic fans. She gave it up, however, because spindly men were routinely hitting on her. Her second breakthrough came when, buoyed by increasing confidence to inhabit a world beyond the life of the sect and the library, she screwed her courage to the sticking place and bought tickets to a live match featuring Cass the Bad Ass and his celebrated opponent Guy "Gorilla" Jones.

The energy of the live ring intoxicated Sophie even from the back row where she had judiciously chosen to sit. In spite of the distance, she could see the sweat shining on the contours of Cassidy's muscles. Awash in a hormonally charged rapture, she nearly wept. That was the first of many live matches she would attend, some of them out of town. "Library conventions," she told Ruth and Lydia. Each time she sat a little closer to the ring and one evening was surprised to find herself in the second row.

Cassidy apparently possessed an unparalleled eye for feminine beauty so even in the midst of a grand performance, he did not overlook this second-row fan. Although brief inattention threw his choreography off slightly, his Bad Ass act was supercharged, his fans roared, Sophie found ecstacy, and they found each other after that match.

Less than a year into the marriage, Sophie's doubts began surfacing. The sweat that could light up rooms (albeit with a borrowed light source) was smelly and sticky. When Cassidy rolled over in bed, it creaked and increasingly seemed on the verge of collapse. And although she had once thought it endearing that he had not been in a library since the fifth grade when Miss Grundy, the school librarian, kicked him out for rowdy behavior, she now thought it pitiful. As Sack listened, a whisker of his memory brushed against the princess, the princess of pea fame, that exquisitely sensitive maiden who slept atop twenty eiderdown mattresses and was bruised by a pea beneath them all. And this maiden, the delicate Sophie, slept next to a large, lumbering man whose simple shifts in bed were disturbing, cataclysmic events. Cassidy was no longer her hero, just a big guy who, she admitted, treated her well. She was desperately disappointed, and after receiving a job promotion, she left him.

In her new position, she actually was sent to library conventions, including one where she met Charles, a man who was everything Cassidy was not—mature, erudite, reserved, dignified, slender and fine boned. "And he is brilliant," she said. "His brilliance shines like the contours of Cassidy's biceps." He romanced her with the poetry of Shakespeare and the Brownings.

When Sack discussed these things—poets, love affairs, feminine beauty—in case consultation, Doppelmann nearly popped with agitated envy. Regis-Rittenhouse said, "It's Sack's case, Doppelmann, get over it. And it's just a case. She didn't jilt you. She doesn't even know who you are."

"Actually," I said, "Sophie does know who Doppelmann is. She confided her waiting-room agitation to Holly, who told me. She was wondering who that older man is who keeps looking at her." Doppelmann is a decade younger than Sack, but was looking a little hangdog after his surgery. Anyway, his behavior shaped up after this comeuppance, but Sack stopped talking about the case. This went on for weeks until I tapped him on the shoulder and reminded him that this is our focus case for heroes et cetera.

Back to the case. In retrospect, Sophie realizes that she had known little about Charles when they married, although she once believed that she had gazed deeply into his soul. Perhaps, but she had not gazed deeply into his domestic situation.

One day a teenager named Virginia stopped by the library to ask about volunteer work there. She had driven in from exurbia and had chosen this library because of its inner-city location where she hoped to inspire less fortunate children to value reading. Sophie chatted with the girl who said she is particularly interested in library work because her father, whom she deeply admires, is a professional librarian. Tonight she would surprise him with her resourcefulness. One shred of information led to another. The oldest of three children, she described her parents as happily married except that her mother is often upset because her father travels much of the time.

At this point she didn't need to ask, but she did. "What's his name?"

"Charles," said Virginia.

Sophie left Charles and plummeted into despair. In that state she presented at FABRCTR. Sack, the wounded healer, had his own despair, which can be helpful: Two despairing people, but only one of them knows that there are two. In this situation it seemed to work out favorably. After Sophie settled into her new and disheartening reality, she and Sack had lengthy discussions about heroes. She read newspaper accounts of firefighters and schoolteachers and biographies of Lysistrada, Margaret Sanger, Gandhi, Martin Luther King and Billie Jean King. She also talked about her father who had been a serious disappointment to both herself and to her mother.

After several months, Sophie pretty much decided that she could live her life without a hero, and Sack decided that he could live his life without being one, which he had done so far anyway. But Sophie would not have known this or anything else about Sack unless she had looked deeply into his soul, which she probably had not and besides, her aptitude for soul rendition is tenuous at best. In the end we were reassured when Sophie became Sophia and Sack dropped that pin-striping nonsense.

END OF CASE

As for heroes and maidens, they have a fragile existence within marriage. And romance? Well, romance has a half life. Although Sack had a successful case, especially with our guidance, we all realize that this area of study has been the one most challenging for our team. We talked it through. In plain language, this topic spooked us. Looking back, it seems as though some little trickster kicked a pile of marbles into our loft. A few of them lodged right in Doppelmann's bladder, and we kept stumbling over the rest.

First of all, Doppelmann regressed to childhood. Nedra took two weeks leave from Copy Tech to care for him even though his surgery was routine. Visiting him in the hospital, I found her reading to him from *The Three Musketeers*. Copies of *Moby Dick* and *Through the Looking-Glass* lay at the foot of his bed. Returning to work in his weakened condition, Doppelmann, who prides himself on his courtly manner, grasp of the hero concept and pre-surgery progress in fencing, became competitive. Now, when you think of a hero, do *you* think of gallstones? No, you don't, and neither does Doppelmann. He wasn't himself. Sack, caught up in adolescent longing as well as protecting his case from the leering Doppelmann, went on the defensive. And Holly was snagged into the Sack-Doppelmann snafu when she was pressed to soothe Sophie.

Bloom became overly protective of herself and everyone else. After all, her daughters are blooming maidens if ever there were, but for how long? She is nervous. We all respect Regis-Rittenhouse's willing acknowledgment of her prejudicial attitudes about heroes, maidens and romance, but that acknowledgment did not prevent her churlish behavior. And I had trouble keeping up with them, documenting all of it and weeding out my ill will because I've had my own excursion through a marriage with an illusory hero and, believe me, he wasn't a beetle collector. Dear reader, our team was out of sorts. In the next chapter we will have a fresh start with a less unsettling topic: infidelity.

Chapter VIII

INFIDELITY AT RISK

We move from heroes and maidens to a related discussion of marital affairs. After all, it is the yearning for these elusive figures, along with ripe opportunity and disappointment in one's predictable, ordinary, inattentive or mean-spirited partner, that culminates in betrayal. If marriage disappears for lack of interest, of course, this is a moot point. The extinction of marriage, an institution which gives life and vitality to marital affairs, would do them in, like sheep extinction to sheep lice. The infidel may be an endangered species.

The end of marriage, however, is not the only threat to the time-honored marital affair. Before we even approached other threats, however, Bloom requested that we address the merits of infidelity. Yes, Bloom did. At this request, Sack roused himself from a mild stupor, Regis-Rittenhouse raised her eyebrows so high they nearly disappeared into her hairline, Doppelmann grinned ghoulishly and I began scrawling the word "merits" large and small all over my notepad. We were listening.

"Of course, we can't go around promoting affairs, but sometimes they reinvigorate marriages that have become tedious and empty," Bloom said, "and due to this very crisis a couple might engage in a meaningful assessment of their relationship, renew their vows, vacation in Tahiti ..."

Yes, we were listening, but each, I suspect, with a third ear. No one took issue with her comments. Personally, I was too distracted by the intriguing fact that it was the choir member who was delivering them that I failed to gather my thoughts enough to form an opinion. Just what pesky little secrets had Bloom been harboring? Hmmm. She had not been to Tahiti lately or ever that I knew, but there was that weekend she and Al spent in the Ozarks.

While repressing a nearly irresistible impulse to ask Bloom a few questions, I suggested that we put her ideas on hold while we explore the perilous future of infidelity. The inveterate marital affair, a mixed bag to be sure, may be in trouble, and we at FABRCTR are the ones to address it. Of all of the destructive forces, the most pernicious, we agreed, is the Internet. Both men and women engage in these virtual affairs, that's right, affairs devoid of skin on skin, bad breath and awkward, frantic disrobing. Put this way Internet infidelity may seem like progress, but Doppelmann put it another way: "Lovely bodies embracing on grassy Wisconsin hillsides, along California surf, atop sweeping mahogany desks. Could all of this be permanently lost to the Internet?" (It's unlikely that Doppelmann has ever had an affair because he so routinely spins fantasies to entertain himself; therefore, he can leave concerns about more probable venues like broom closets, bathroom stalls and lapsing motels to the less fanciful.) Just as he was about to launch into keening, Regis-Rittenhouse reminded him that marital affairs are still abundant and have not yet lost their desperate, high-pitched, emotionally intense quality. He admitted that he had briefly lost sight of this and settled down.

But it is true. With the onset of virtual affairs, a richly romantic literary and royal tradition faces an impoverished future. While this may solve some problems like the elimination of sexually transmitted diseases, unwanted pregnancies and stray earrings, who will be the Madame Bovary, the Anna Karenina, the Prince Charles of the future? The Internet infidel is settling for oh so much less. We unanimously agreed that this poses a serious threat to the flesh-and-blood encounters of illicit lovers.

"Public education about the body and the brain is another threat to infidelity," Bloom pointed out. "Look at what happened to all of the smokers after we learned about the impact of smoking on the lungs and the heart."

"Yeah," said Sack, who excused himself and went outside for a cigarette. (He had nearly forgotten his regular break.)

"When people are informed, they change their habits," Bloom continued. "If they know that they are just seduced into infidelity by a maelstrom of hormones, the same ones that coupled them with their disappointing partners, they'll be more objective." She had a point (and she had more credibility with me now that I knew she might be talking from in vivo experience), but then again objectivity is very rare. Ego, hunger, aggression, hormones, nicotine depletion … so many obstacles.

We went ahead and imagined a rational, objective approach anyway. It might go something like this: While experiencing a rising tide of hormonal activity in the company of a potential lover, a married person might say, "Oh, isn't this interesting? In the presence of this human being, I am flooded with euphoria, exhilaration and massive sensations in my genital area, but I am completely in control because I know that this is the work of my hormones, those little tricksters, and that this person is not divine but an ordinary, defective, perhaps even tedious individual who undoubtedly has unseemly and annoying habits." Further, the married person would fully realize that such feelings will dissipate before the year's end unless the two maintain a highly pitched intrigue. Barriers, separations and secrecy, of course, nourish infidelity and sustain such a pitch. Unless this results in a permanent disconnection or the couple moves on to other entertainment, the hormones are only enlivened and encouraged to work ever harder, like the child weakling who through indefatigable effort matures into a square-shouldered Army general.

Hormones are not sensitive to social issues and personal complications, so they will work assiduously for the infidel. You see, they do not know whether you are married or not, and they would not care if they did know. Knowing and caring is not part of their job description. They are just fulfilling their function like rain clouds do when they let loose on a locale that had a downpour of biblical proportions only the day before. Whether floods, crop devastation or outdoor weddings, rain clouds do not care. Out of the same sheer ignorance and detachment, hormones never discourage infidelity.

People may come to realize this and refuse to be fooled. They could learn to ignore their hormones like they learn to ignore their smoke alarm when they know it is just signaling the usual combination of over-charred salmon and a slightly dysfunctional exhaust system. Doppelmann did not think that people could learn any such thing, that mere information is not enough. He suggested that in addition to the biological facts, people would need some help with disembodiment. Since the body is inclined to be such a nuisance, a partner, in the interest of being faithful, might want to learn how to transmigrate into an ethereal state of some sort.

We politely listened until Bloom pointed out that we had not finished enumerating the threats to the survival of infidelity and that no one had even mentioned Viagra. That startled us because we should have been on top of it, but it wasn't too late. After pooling our collection of reportage, hearsay, facts and experiences with the pill, we decided that it cuts both ways. If more men use Viagra within their marriages, their wives will be less likely to wander. However, some men can become so confident about their renewed prowess that they will be more likely to wander. This, in fact, has led to a staggering reversal of fortune for far too many men. Pushed beyond their natural limits, dozens have perished at the orgasmic instant of their extra-marital embrace. Puzzling as it is, very few men using Viagra within the marital situation have faced the same fate. If they are more likely to expire using it outside of the marriage than inside, infidelity will never survive. Philandering males will either die off or avoid these encounters entirely. We are sensitive to this data which may need further analysis. (Sack returned from his cigarette break.)

Regis-Rittenhouse had had enough. "Monogamy is an unnatural state. Infidelity is not going anywhere. It lives. Even if there weren't any marriages, it would survive. Since infidels are going to be around, let's just regulate infidelity," she said, then paused. An idea was gestating; a mischievous grin surfaced. Then she continued, "Yes, let's regulate infidelity. This might fit nicely into an existing agency, maybe the Bureau of Alcohol, Tobacco and Firearms. We could just add Infidelity and call the whole thing ATFI or FATI or FIAT or whatever."

The team agreed that we did not really want to subject an innocent populace to government surveillance of its personal business, but that such a regulation would be perfect for elected officials. "All of them," Regis-Rittenhouse said, "from the county sheriff to the president."

We sketched out a workable plan: Each elected individual would be allowed one extramarital encounter a year. He would have to register the encounter, like a handgun. If he ignored that regulation, he would be denied access to future extramarital encounters. The plan would not only eliminate the extended agony of the wives of elected officials—we couldn't think of any husbands similarly injured—but it would eliminate endless investigations and reduce government spending. As we were congratulating ourselves on our latest innovative idea, Bloom reminded us that social policy is beyond the scope of our current study.

Then just what is the scope of our study, we all wondered. Perhaps it was time for a case study. "There are too many infidelity cases and they're all the same," grumbled

Regis-Rittenhouse. She was crabby because we had dropped her idea.

"Oh no," said Doppelmann, "each one has its own lyric and narrative arc, its own pathos, its own exaltation. The players writhe in pain, soar in passion, flounder in despair and disappointment. And each one does it in his or her own unique way."

"They may be exhilarating or ruinous for the players," Regis-Rittenhouse replied, "but they're yawners for me. Look." She was back at the whiteboard where, with the help of our team, she reduced infidelity, not to one, but to three types:

The Cherry Bomb: *Bored, disappointed or unsuspecting partner> Meets appealing interested person> Hormones activate> Affair ensues> Partner finds out> Chaos, tears, anger> Sort it out with therapist> Leave marriage or stay in marriage.*

The Cumbersome Conscience: *Bored, disappointed or unsuspecting partner> Meets appealing interested person> Hormones activate> Affair ensues> Partner does not find out> Unilateral chaos, heartache, confusion> Talk to therapist about it> Leave marriage or stay in marriage.*

The Shrug: *Bored, disappointed or unsuspecting partner> Meets appealing interested person> Hormones activate> Affair ensues> Partner does not find out> Affair continues or peters out> Marriage stays intact.*

Even Doppelmann agreed that stripped to the bone, this is about how it goes. And Sack said, "If it were not for discovery in the Cherry Bomb Type and guilt in the Cumbersome Conscience Type, we could just forget about affairs altogether and our business would be cut in half."

"I would rue the day," Doppelmann said. "Torn blouses, lost stockings, clandestine embraces, frantic phone calls, sex, lies and videotape." Doppelmann's imagery notwithstanding, Sack's insight did not go unheeded. Sack is actually quite insightful. Nicotine helps. Brainstorming at FABRCTR takes a hit when he is on one of his quit-smoking gigs. He was right; discovery and guilt are often the fuel which drives our couples right into our church. A closer look was in order.

Discovery has many variations. A gulled partner (GP, see Glossary) might find out about the offending partner's affair (OP, see Glossary) because he simply confesses. This is passive discovery and calls for very little discernment or guile on the part of the GP unless, of course, she has been astute enough to notice his growing interest in cologne and tanning salons and begins to ask probing questions. This often confounds the OP who cannot think of anything to say but the truth. In the tougher cases a long devotion to law and order television programs emboldens the GP to use more aggressive means to extract a confession. In any case, woe to both partners. The truth does not set them free, at least not just yet. It just dumps two goldfish into the rinse cycle.

More complex discovery requires espionage. Sometimes this merely involves filching telephone bills, perusing credit card bills and sniffing clothing. Some GP's stalk the OP, but the more affluent hire a detective to do the stalking. A Doppelmann case demonstrates what an inventive and tortured partner can do in a Cherry Bomb case, and following that, a Sack case demonstrates how a partner tortures himself in a Cumbersome Conscience case.

Rick and Helen

This couple had been married for eleven years when they sought help at FABRCTR. The cherry bomb had exploded, and Rick remained deeply wounded by Helen's affair.

Doppelmann took a history of the couple. Rick's first misfortune was that his parents had named him Hector after the Trojan War hero. A clever boy, by second grade he had convinced everyone to call him Rick, after Ranger Rick. Still known as Rick when he entered college, he told friends that he was the namesake of the Humphrey Bogart character in *Casablanca*. His second misfortune was that Helen had perceived him as a hero when they met. Because he was socially charming and attractive to her friends, she was convinced that he could do anything. (Her friends were especially difficult to please.) For his part, Rick had long aspired to marry a lovely woman named Helen and here she was, in the form of a schoolteacher. Yet he still admitted to no one, not even to Helen, that his given name was Hector. None of his gregarious friends would understand the bookish nature of his family background, and he feared that they would roast him mercilessly were they to discover it. But he could safely marry her without anyone making the association to the ancient city of Troy.

The first few years of their marriage went quite smoothly for the couple as they fell into habits and rituals conducive to domesticity. As time went on, however, Rick revealed a growing tendency to manage more than just social impressions, particularly after their daughter Sydney was born. He began editing Helen's grocery lists and selecting underwear and socks for both of them. Helen cringed at this growing tendency which she saw as seriously encroaching on her own freedom as well

135

as her daughter's. It tapped the latent streak of opposition in her nature, and she began surreptitiously breaking his rules. About the time Sydney was eight years old, for example, he forbade the girl to watch sitcoms, so when he was out, Helen and Sydney snuggled up and, as complicit as two ten-year olds smoking behind the garage, they watched three or four, back to back.

The big rule that she broke, however, was one Rick never thought to make. Helen began to fraternize with Santiago, an adorable Latin American man, somewhat her junior, with one pierced ear. Because he was part of the school's technical support staff, he frequently came around to help her out. They would discuss all manner of things which began with computer esoterica and quickly evolved into Helen's marital disappointments. Santiago, single, was a divine listener according to Helen's later accounts. He had his own mating problems and, of course, both were certain that they had now found the only individual extant who would ever understand them. Eventually they would embrace, sometimes upon Helen's laminated table, a cast-off from the lunchroom. (No sweeping mahogany desks at Garfield Middle School. Doppelmann was disappointed.)

Meanwhile Rick, who was, by the way, still perfectly charming in the company of Helen's friends, became increasingly suspicious. Helen was a little too distant, a little too sunny and a little too frequently detained at school. He had had a brief fling himself in the early part of their marriage (the Shrug Type), so he was not clueless regarding these matters. But this was definitely something he was not managing. Drawing from childhood memories, he made a plan.

His parents had raised young Hector on the story of the Trojan War. They began telling him parts of the classic when he was three years old, read him a child's version when he was five and an entire translation of *The Iliad* when he was eight. Rick had married a Helen and now he would do the rest. One morning she mentioned that she would be home late because a new file was being delivered to her classroom after school hours. Rick rapidly pulled his plan together. He called his buddy Aggie who ran a small trucking company. Deftly managing his image even if it meant deceiving an accommodating friend, he told Aggie that he wanted to surprise Helen because it was her birthday. Aggie said great and asked a couple of his guys to put Rick in a crate and deliver it to Helen's classroom at the appointed time.

So Rick went over to Ace Trucking, got himself wedged inside a credible file box and bumped along in the back of the truck. As instructed, the haulers dumped it just outside of Helen's classroom. Sure enough, Helen and Santiago were there and clearly puzzled by the arrival of this box. (Helen had forgotten today's ploy.) They let it sit while they caught up on one another's day. Meanwhile Rick became increasingly uncomfortable with his wedged-in status. His legs were cramping up and anxiety was pressing against his bladder. He desperately needed a bathroom break. What had all those guys in the Trojan horse done about these things? Maybe the horse's interior architecture included a relief station, a stretching area and even a little wine bar. He had never given any thought to creature comforts inside that horse, not even after he studied *The Iliad* in college (which he had done at the behest of his parents, but concealed from everyone else. This was not particularly difficult because none of his fraternity brothers had ever ventured near the classics department.)

Meanwhile, Helen and Santiago were talking, but whatever they were doing seemed of secondary importance right now. In fact, they had nearly vanished from Rick's radar screen. If he were paying attention, he might have expected the two of them to moan in the throes of love making. But it was he who moaned and it was hardly amorous. In fact he had to shout, "I'm dying in here! Let me out!" He had not expected it to go like this, but then neither had Helen and Santiago. Helen found her box cutter and Santiago ripped the carton open. Rick jumped out, startling both of them, then sprinted down the hall to the boys' lavatory. Santiago had the wit to leave immediately. Rick relieved himself, returned, slumped in one of the student desks, put his head down, then slowly lifted it and peered up at Helen.

The next week they came to FABRCTR. Helen agreed to stop seeing Santiago, although at first she was a little slippery about it. Upon hearing that Rick was replicating the Greek classic, she briefly had a renewed sense of Rick's heroism and basked in her ordained role as the beautiful and hotly pursued Helen of Troy. And as for the saga of his early indoctrination and unflagging efforts to hide it from others, she felt compassion and caring. "Poor Ricky," she said. "Why didn't you share this with me years ago?"

END OF CASE

We complimented Doppelmann on the fine job he had done with this couple. Even caught up in a romance of classic proportions, our Doppelmann can be clear-headed about the basics. Rick loosened up, and Helen matured beyond her adolescent insurgency and switched to another school the following year. Sydney was surprised by her father's occasional companionship during sitcoms. And somewhat put off. She lost interest and moved on to the Internet where she chatted with friends for one half hour after another.

The case of Rick and Helen remains one of FABRCTR's finest examples of the Cherry Bomb type, and it has the added colorful feature of espionage in the service of exposing infidelity. In our second case, the Cumbersome Conscience type, it is guilt and not discovery that fuels the marital action. As fortune would have it, Sack, our resident expert on guilt, had the perfect case.

Before we begin, however, I need to warn the reader of potential bias. Sack's case involves a minister. This would hardly need special attention except that our Sack, generally an open-minded individual—as open-minded as anyone you might know—sees ministers as falling into two distinct categories: Machiavellian or Savagely Scrupulous. Since we have been unable to disabuse him of this unsavory polarity, we have accepted this as a quirk, or possibly a counter-quirk, that we must live with. Perhaps it has something to do with his experiences in the church of his youth. Whatever the origins of his prejudicial thinking, we are obliged to steer him away from the ministers who come to FABRCTR for help. However, when Francis, a Lutheran minister, came for his intake interview, he fudged and said that he was an administrator for homeless shelters. That's why the case slipped through the cracks and went to Sack. Fortunately, however, Francis falls into the Savagely Scrupulous category. This is not necessarily fortunate for Francis, but it was for Sack who carries marked antipathy for Machiavellian persons of the cloth.

Francis and Anne

Francis had been married to Anne for 25 years when he came to FABRCTR alone. Also the daughter of a minister, Anne, like her mother, had been the proverbial dutiful wife; she had stood by Francis during divinity school and his various ministries. Included in his congregation's current ministries is the administration of the Heart and Hands Homeless Shelter, so Francis was only mildly disingenuous during the intake interview. Although the church hired a social worker to oversee the shelter, Francis remains actively engaged in its affairs. Every Wednesday he spends the night there during which time he checks in the homeless, joins them for a stew or macaroni and cheese dinner and arouses them in the morning. Not only does he enjoy talking with members of this eclectic group, but he finds them a rich source of sermon material.

Some of the homeless are women. Francis became particularly engaged with one of them, Caprice. She had come to the city from a rural area where she had been raised in a trailer while step-siblings, half-siblings, uncles, parents, stepparents and miscellaneous wayfarers of unknown origin rotated in and out. At first she supported herself by sweeping floors at a fledgling medical devices company. Since it had only a handful of employees and Caprice, in spite of her unfortunate name, demonstrated industry and reliability, her employer gave her increasing responsibilities with pay raises to match. In a few years she was able to purchase a small townhouse. A year later it burned down, her employer's company folded as did her insurance company, all of which left her on the streets. She was starting over at Heart and Hands.

Francis found it remarkable that she was able to overcome her chaotic childhood, lamented her current misfortunes and became increasingly intrigued by her deep, moody gaze. Anne, after all, had become too independent in recent years. It's true, the children were now young adults and rarely home, but she was apparently exhibiting a fresh sense of freedom and accomplishment. "She is a member of three boards, none of them even related to church activities," he told Sack. "Planned Parenthood, a women's political campaign fundraising group and some sort of court thing … volunteers watchdog judges presiding over domestic abuse cases. Stuff like that."

Francis found many reasons to visit the shelter during the month of Caprice's stay. Meanwhile, Anne was delighted with his intensified interest in it. She considers the shelter a refreshing break for Francis who shoulders the demoralizing burden of church politics. For Francis, Caprice was oh so much more than a break: She was a lovely, vulnerable creature who stared deeply into his eyes and mesmerized him with her heartrending narratives. Night and day she moved like a sprite through his imagination. An obsession worthy of the saints colonized his entire being.

When Caprice was able to leave the shelter for more permanent housing, he arranged coffee dates and once they went to a movie together. Francis had never touched her, however, but for hugs upon greetings and departures. Now his longing for that touch had reached cataclysmic proportions. After a tryst in which they had their first kiss—a kiss for all seasons—he went home and had very good sex with Anne, but it was Caprice who was in his embrace.

Francis was not a man to take any of this lightly. He judged his feelings as wrong and his behavior unacceptable. While he had not engaged in adultery in the literal sense, adulterous thoughts consumed him. He prayed and asked for forgiveness for his thoughts, his feelings and especially for The Kiss. He prayed in his own church, he prayed in the Temple of Aaron, he prayed at the Friends Meeting House, he prayed on the banks of the Mississippi River. His prayers, however, were not eradicating his all-consuming lust, so he tried torture. From beneath the floorboards of the attic, he retrieved his hair shirt—unused since the days following a college drinking binge—put it on and crept up to one of the children's empty rooms for a fitful night's sleep. Still he felt no better. For the first time in his life, he wished he were a Catholic; confessing to a priest would be easier than confessing to Anne. Then he remembered Father Patrick, a friend he had made while serving on an ecumenical committee. The two met for a beer and Francis did, in fact, confess to Father Patrick, who was quite understanding and referred him to FABRCTR.

After a few sessions, to Francis' mortification, Sack suggested that he talk to Anne about the affair. Immediately it looked to Sack as though Francis couldn't catch any air. Had the man stopped breathing? Sack stared at him a moment while he considered administering CPR. But Francis came around and managed to say that he would prefer praying with Sack or at the very least expanding the discussion of his agonizing guilt; Sack preferred that he tell Anne. When he did, he was relieved, but also surprised and mildly disappointed that she took it so calmly. "She has the name of a saint, but she doesn't have to act like one," he later told Sack. Then he became suspicious; maybe she was so unreasonably calm because she had had her own affair. He asked her.

"No," she said, "but it's not as if I can't imagine it." He was unsettled by her comment and wondered if her conscience was just a might patchy.

Anne and Francis came together to see Sack a few times, then completed their business. Anne accepted Francis' dalliance and said that she would be somewhat more attentive to him and his congregation, but added that she would be unlikely to duplicate the deep, moody gaze of the now legendary Caprice.

END OF CASE

Persons burdened with a Cumbersome Conscience tend to avoid affairs altogether. The agony can be overwhelming, and like Francis, they may be slow to forgive themselves. He still stops by periodically to have a talk with Sack about it, and once in a while he and Father Patrick meet in a local pub where they consult with one another about the infidelity of various parishioners who seek their help as a result of discovery or guilt.

As for the third infidelity type, the Shrug, our team has little to say. We only learn about this type indirectly when someone comes to FABRCTR for something else, something like Hair Loss Anxiety, Wrinkle Despair or Imposter Syndrome. One of these individuals may mention an old affair in an off-handed way, the way he might mention a nearly forgotten night at the casino: "Oh, yeah, one time I was up $1500, but lost $20 for the night."

Except for Doppelmann we agreed that the strongest case we could make for affairs is that they are good for business the way hernias and broken limbs are good for a physician's business. This does not mean, dear reader, that we wish them upon you, but some of you may wish them upon yourselves. One may just pop up in your life, hormone education notwithstanding.

Chapter IX

THE USUSAL SUSPECTS:
IN-LAWS AND STEPCHILDREN

Humans share over 97% of their genes with the common mouse, yet married persons often insist that they share less than 5% of their genes with their incidentally acquired kin: in-laws and stepchildren. When asked to explain this discrepancy, a partner may produce a glazed stare or a tale as convoluted as a politician's defense of his budget policy. Perhaps he or she fails to grasp the significance of this fact for it means that mice, in-laws, stepchildren and humans share a common ancestor. What's more, each human carries the gene for a tail. Scientists tell us that they could activate this gene to create tails in humans. "They can just skip it," says Regis-Rittenhouse. "I had a brother-in-law once. He already had a tail."

This attitude may have its roots in some primal need to protect one's own tribe and to justify its deeds. When partners resort to case-building, that is, inventing reasons why one's bloodline is superior to that of one's mate, trouble ensues:

Comparisons are made, competitions created, days wasted, emotions spent, holidays forsaken. Arranged marriages prevent many of these problems. Families who arrange marriages know one another, share a similar position in the hierarchy of the culture or exchange money and property for a person, so they have respect for in-laws, and stepchildren are rare. Peace is made; complaints silenced. Nevertheless, couples today will have none of it. Young and old alike insist on selecting their own mates, and marriage counselors prosper.

The reputation of in-laws is so poor that singles will trumpet the absence of parents or siblings in ads:

Baggage-Free
Hoping to find woman who enjoys golf, tennis, jazz,
travel and a good movie and who wants to share
love and companionship with attractive, charming,
affectionate 38 year old SWM whose parents are
permanently living in Antarctica.

A single person may say these things even if they are not true, or he may omit pertinent information. Perhaps his parents actually do live in Antarctica, but he does not note that he has an overbearing sister who writes a weekly advice column on relationships or that he has four children. (Marriages can be as hobbled by stepchildren as by in-laws. We'll get to stepchildren later.)

As noted in our first chapter, the individual differences of two besotted people are often muted during courtship.[11] If all goes well—you've probably done it yourself—you meet the family. The first visit foreshadows the unbearable unlikeness

---

[11]Our team admits that courtship is a quaint concept, but that it nevertheless continues to have merit.

of being you will encounter after you are married. It's true that these people are strangers, but they are also strange, and their homes are even stranger. There are booming voices, curious odors and shrill music. Their weaselly little terrier is unfriendly, they arrange their furniture at odd angles, and they gossip about the neighbors too much or not enough. Your potential brother-in-law operates a Caterpillar at work, and it sticks in your mind. You've never known anyone who did anything like that, and now you have lost the ability to envision a caterpillar as simply a pudgy worm; no, it's also a sort of mechanical T-rex. Your future sister-in-law seems to have had a husband at one time, but no one knows where he went, or if in fact, he has gone anywhere. No one ever asks. The world of these people is a surreal one, a tropical forest where leaves are larger than elephant ears, and monkeys are screeching, but you can't hear them. You're part Goldilocks, part Alice. You've lost your innocence.

Amazingly enough, these experiences discourage very few single people from moving forward in the relationship. If they think about it at all, they resort to denial or to specious reasoning:

Denial: *"Those people hardly exist, and we will rarely see them once we are married."*

Specious Reasoning, Mutation Type: *"My future partner is a fine example of a biological mutation, and he will carry through with none of the unseemly characteristics of his family, especially with my excellent input."*

Specious Reasoning, Phoenix Type: *"Examples abound of the charming or gifted individual who rises like a phoenix from the ashes of a disagreeable or disordered family: Eugene O'Neill, Marilyn Monroe, Cinderella."*

Hence, uneasiness is subverted. With their cognitive dissonance under control, the couple marries. Each becomes better acquainted with the in-laws and often adapts to their idiosyncratic modes of communication. For example, when Joe and Shelley visit her parents and Joe's father-in-law asks that he and Shelley stay longer, he means it; when his mother-in-law asks the same thing, she doesn't mean it, except if it's Thursday night when she wants to watch *ER* and her husband will insist on the comedy channel or some other cable thing even though he knows how much she loves ER and she shouldn't have to watch it in the kitchen because the set there is so small and the kitchen has no stuffed chairs anyway but she knows he will watch *ER* without bellyaching if Joe and Shelley stay longer because they are guests and they both like *ER*. Because his mother-in-law never says these things directly, Joe has worked hard to master this Rubik's Cube of communication. Shelley is of some help, but the networks are of no help when they scramble their programming. Then he has to start all over.

For those like Joe who actually do adapt to their in-laws, these experiences are generally not suffered in silence, and if the noise isn't prenuptial, it begins early in the marriage. Persons who find increasing discomfort with their new families may discover an altruistic side to their nature; instead of spending holidays with the family, they will spend them in soup kitchens where they feed the homeless.[12] But it is difficult to avoid in-laws altogether. There are weddings, graduations and funerals, and even if unseen, a partner's family members often pervade everyday life. *Little remarks,* disguised as

---

[12]The neglected in-laws believe that this altruism is exaggerated.

mere observations, are grievances and often copiously made. The reader may remember Fritz's dishwasher-stacking quirk and Lizzie's tendency to implicate his mother in the annoying habit. The poor, maligned woman lives 2000 miles from the couple, but she inhabits their kitchen almost daily. Our team reports other typical comments:

"Your dad never helps around the house either, and he doesn't even *know* where the dustbuster is kept," and

"It's *soooo* annoying when you pop your gum and your alcoholic brother *does the same thing*," and

"That's the same bitchy tone your sister uses when she can't find *her* mascara."

A partner can become hypersensitive to these comments and develop an uncanny ability to spot judgement, even where none exists. For example, when Lizzie mentions a hyena or house fly in the context of a TV nature special, Fritz whooshes it out of context and says, "You're always picking on my mom."

After we had discussed these things in the loft, Bloom pointed out that not all in-laws are misbegotten or annoying and that some of them are really quite lovely.

"None of them are lovely," said Regis-Rittenhouse. "You mean, some of them are *tolerable*."

"Well, we are all in-laws to someone, and we're not so bad," Bloom said.

"Not me," said Regis-Rittenhouse. "I am no one's in-law. What's more, I wouldn't be caught having one. They have a dreadful reputation."

Doppelmann and Sack came to Bloom's rescue. They argued with Regis-Rittenhouse who gradually backed off and then covered her tracks with an idea: "Well, so all in-laws are not the same, and some are not even reprehensible, so let's sort out their differences and create another typology." We all became quite enthusiastic about this project, but Dopplemann said that the word type is too dry to use for so variegated a group as in-laws and suggested that we refer to the types as *species*. Sack said the word species sounds too biological, but the rest of us liked it, so Dopplemann prevailed. We had all listened to hundreds of in-law complaints over the years and pooled our respective experiences to come up with this speciology, the first of its kind:

In-law Species

Aspiring Roommates: These in-laws are generally quite pleased to have someone new in the family because of the opportunity they provide: another family pad opens up. If the door is left ajar even a micrometer, one of this species moves right in, plunders the refrigerator, borrows money and stays too long. "It's family after all, and isn't this what families are for?" he reasons. While lodging with you, he may take sides in your marital quarrels and consider it a favor. More commonly, in a fit of largesse, he shows his appreciation by sharing his recently delivered pizza with you. Otherwise, he expects that you or your mate have the clairvoyance to stock the cupboards and refrigerator with his preferred food and drink.

An Aspiring Roommate who does not achieve what he aspires to be—a family roommate—is less lucky. We have a few pointers that will increase that probability. Relocating rarely works because this species is geographically quite flexible. Instead, we recommend that you buy a malamute or charge a hefty rent. Although the latter may be the most effective way to foil his plans, be on guard. He just may agree to an outrageously high rate, but any agreement will soon disappear in the crush of his other bills. Those pizzas add up.

Members of this species rarely send thank-you notes.

Cheerful Rubes: The world of the Cheerful Rube is clear and certain; they are tidy-minded people. These in-laws, however, may not be as clueless (or even as cheerful) as they seem. It's hard to tell because they appear to do the right thing by you, but invariably miss. They follow contact sports, smack smiley faces on their bumpers or refrigerators and attend mass prayer services at the Mall of America. For some of you one of this species makes a fine in-law, but if you consider yourself a nuanced thinker with highly developed sensibilities and a roiling inner life, a Cheerful Rube is the worst kind. In dealing with this species, we recommend metronomic head nods, although that may not be enough for more complicated situations. For example, if your mother-in-law calls to invite you two for dinner and says, "Just come at the usual time," and there is no usual time, you ask:

"What time?"

"Oh, the usual time is just fine."

"What is the usual time?"

"Well, whatever works for you."

"Seven o'clock."

"Now, honey, that's way too late for us. Roy gets a little crabby, you know, if he has to wait too long for dinner."

"Five-thirty."

"Now, that's a little early."

We particularly want to warn persons living in the Midwest about this species because a majority of this species congregates here. Beware the Cheerful Rube.

Crustaceans: Unless you are a direct descendent of either royalty or Cary Grant, a Crustacean will see you, a fledgling family member, as an interloper. Our team calls this species Crustaceans because like barnacles and wood lice, they have a shell that protects them from the less attractive realities about themselves. Here's how they see things: Theirs is a well-bred, well-educated and well-endowed family, and now a blundering bumpkin like you has come along and punched a hole in their souffle. (Go wash your hands, young man. Don't you know your place?) You will be uncomfortable with these people, challenged and never quite trusted. After all, you have abducted one of their own and at any time could perform another, equally reprehensible act. They are on guard. And you should be too.

One subspecies of this group is merely sententious; another is overbearing and intrusive. If you host a family baby shower, for example, the overbearing subspecies will insist on bringing the entire meal or having it catered, apparently because of your ineptitude or boorishness. One way to handle this is to invite a few boisterous neighbors; another is to leave the dog's mess in the middle of the living room floor. Guilty little pleasures.

With the Crustaceans, it is judicious to be modest because they will not brook your successes. For instance, you may expect them to be proud of a daughter-in-law who is the marketing vice-president of a major bank. To this the Crustacean says:

"These days that bank is letting *anybody* in," or

"The bank's CEO is a crook," or

"It's not the same as an academic position."

And if you become chair of the English department:

"Third-rate university."

Downplay your successes and don't forget about the homeless on holidays.

Nannies: In naming this species, we are using the term nanny generically. Not only do these in-laws babysit, they also fix plumbing, change storm windows and fetch dry cleaning— all for you and your partner. These may sound like in-laws the Pope might beatify, but there are risks. They can become presumptuous and officious, and you will put up with it because of the perks and hate yourself for it. Warm, gracious and unintrusive Nannies can present another kind of problem. If your spouse becomes intolerable, you two have grown distant or she is having an affair, and you want to leave her, you're caught. You have come to prefer her family members substantially more than you prefer her, or for that matter, more than you prefer your own family members, and you don't want to give them up. Horns of a Dilemma.

Phantoms: This is the vanishing species of in-law. No, they are not vanishing in the ecological sense; they just vanish from the lives of their adult children. They can hardly be found. As already noted, some individuals use this situation as a marketing device during courting. (By the way, this can be ill-advised because an occasional potential partner is actually looking for some folks who might be an improvement over her own family.) These in-laws may be teaching English to the Inuits in the Arctic Circle, they may have taken an infinite RV excursion around North America and occasionally drop a postcard from somewhere like Baffin Bay, Daytona Beach or Waco, or maybe one of them is a serious introvert who reads Emily Dickinson or H. L. Mencken in a cramped little room just down the block from you. There are many ways of vanishing; it is an art form. If this is what your in-laws do, we recommend that you don't take it personally.[13] They may always have been this way and are not necessarily trying to avoid you.

Reprobates: This species of in-law is often more troubling than the others. Before you were married, you had never met a person who was serving a prison sentence, but now ... *no* degrees of separation. It's true that your brother-in-law will be released in only six months, but he expects to be picked up in a limousine so he can "go out in class." (You figure this must be a convict thing.) Especially unsettling is that you didn't know this man existed before he became your brother-in-law, but everything about this family is unsettling. When they all come to visit, they cross your threshold like a thundering herd of cattle, settle into a mild uproar, spill beer and eat voraciously. (Apparently, they don't use forks.) If you have occasion to stay at their house, they feed you plenty and put you up in the gun room. As you look back to the period of your engagement, you can remember evidence that you so adroitly overlooked. You knew that your betrothed's aging parents annually ride their

---

[13]Although it often is personal.

Harleys to Sturgis for the big bike jamboree, but you considered it spunky, even hip. Now the spunky is buried somewhere in the Black Hills, and the hip has been shot into space. At any time you expect a time-traveling Neanderthal to show up and claim to be your wife's uncle.

END OF SPECIOLOGY

Although some individuals report that they are quite fond of their in-laws and that their spouses have reasonable parents and evolved siblings—although even then, there is bound to be at least one windbag among the cousins—others, perhaps yourself, need some help coping with it. Whatever species your in-laws,[14] remember that you are not alone in your plight. Even if you think your case is unique, thousands have gone before you. If this thought isn't enough to boost your morale, you may want to form an in-law support group.

In terms of managing these relationships on a day-to-day basis, we suggest that you apply the finesse of James Bond along with the tact of Miss Manners, rather than the confrontation of Godzilla, although our team is sensitive to the difficulty of maintaining finesse and tact while an ex-con wearing a halo of entitlement is raiding your refrigerator. Also, while discussing these issues with your mate, remember to use a harmonic tone while avoiding high-pitched, atonal and repetitive speech. Bloom wishes to remind the reader again that if you have even one in-law, you *are* an in-law. While this is a sobering thought, it is also true and worth remembering because it may keep your arrogance in check.

---

[14]Readers are encouraged to add to our speciology in case our team has overlooked a significant species. No one has paved our way so we look to you for assistance. Our cutting-edge position does have its hazards.

Stepchildren

If the reputation of in-laws is bad, that of stepmothers is worse. The Cinderella story has done no favor for this class of individuals, but for couples who blend families, it is the stepchildren who defy sympathy. Like in-laws, they are *different.* They have odd little habits, they're spoiled and whiney and they're, well, not as bright as your own children. The off button on the TV remote is more elusive to them than Bigfoot. And while staying with their other set of parents, they call to request lunch money.

If you're planning to have stepchildren, we suggest that you begin the relationship before they are toilet trained or wait until they are eligible to vote. In between you won't fare well. Avoid especially the teenage years because these young people are already peevish, and if you make suggestions or requests, they might just snap your head right off. The last thing they need is another full-grown person to boss them around, especially some Johnny-come-lately parent. The FABRCTR team suggests that during these middle years, you delay your plans for a second or third marriage, find someone less encumbered or just meet your betrothed annually on a beach somewhere. Maui is good. Curacao and so on.

Couples with blended families have not been among our most successful cases. Although the following Regis-Rittenhouse case is somewhat atypical and its main player more annoying than most of our clientele, we selected it to help you see that the greatest hazard of the blended family is its failure to blend.

Bucky and Jasmine

Bucky, 42, and Jasmine, 32, married for just under a year, presented at FABRCTR in their gym clothes. Ken and Barbie with bloated biceps. The two met when Bucky was married to Elise and his three children were ages 3, 7 and 9. Jasmine, his personal trainer, had been single for several years. She had two children, then ages 8 and 11. The couple fell in love near the free weights. After a year-long affair, Bucky divorced Elise and married Jasmine. He says he knew from the start that he would never want his children co-mingling with hers, so they married with the stipulation that the children would never meet. (Apparently Bucky had never attended a pre-school where sharing is emphasized.) Perhaps either desperate or blinded by romance, Jasmine agreed to this, although she now says she doesn't remember doing so.

When Regis-Rittenhouse asked Bucky why he left his first wife, he said, "I left for passion and purpose, to discover my personal truth, to live my life deliberately, to get my needs met and to marry the woman I love."

She challenged the testosterone-infested fuzzy forest of his mind: "You left because you had the hots for Jasmine."

"You're harsh," said Bucky.

"Yes, I am," she said.

Now the marital passion was dimming, and the two were at loggerheads about the agreement Bucky swears they had made. Keeping the children apart was keeping Jasmine and Bucky apart. Of Bucky's children, Jasmine had met only Kennedy who had occasionally accompanied Bucky to the gym before her parents divorced; none of them knew he had remarried. And Jasmine's children, Sam and Lucy, didn't know about Bucky's children. Even though he was now living with them and he was officially their stepfather, they were hardly warming up to this guy who was about as cuddly as a crab and playful as a prison guard. (He kept his distance.) He had rented a little apartment in a large complex with a swimming pool that neither Jasmine nor her children ever saw. Every other weekend he stayed there with his own children. After splashing around in the pool, they all went off to the movies or the mall. But together or not, it was the insult that hurt Jasmine the most. "What's wrong with my children?" she repeatedly asked.

The whole matter had come to a head shortly before the two came to FABRCTR. Bucky and his children were filing out of the cineplex where they had just seen *Monsters, Inc.* when his oldest child Kennedy tugged at his jacket. She had just spotted Jasmine. "Hey, Dad, there's your friend Jasmine from the gym, and she's got kids with her. Let's go talk to her," she said, then dashed across the lobby to greet her before Bucky could protest. He awkwardly hung back, but the younger children, McKenzie and Bucky Junior, followed her. When Bucky Senior finally shuffled over, he cooly greeted Jasmine and her children. (Sam and Lucy had assumed he was out of town again.) The irrepressible Kennedy said, "Let's all go get ice cream together." Bucky said no, but Kennedy's enthusiasm infected the other children, and she prevailed. Bucky apparently suffered through the excursion, but averted further contact even though Kennedy invited Sam and Lucy to come over to their dad's place for a swim.

Jasmine saw this chance meeting as a breakthrough; after all, the children seemed to like one another, and surely

Bucky could see how much easier it would be just to go with it. Nevertheless, he held steadfastly to the original—perhaps apocryphal—agreement. So now, with Regis-Rittenhouse as witness, Jasmine asked Bucky again: "What's wrong with my children?"

Both women looked at Bucky. He stuttered, stammered and prevaricated. "They're just not … you know."

"No, I don't know," Jasmine said.

"Well, Sam is … he bites other children."

"What? Once, when he was three years old."

"And Lucy, she's too mature for her age. She wears lipstick and those little halter tops. She's just too, too … alluring." (Our team gives credit to Regis-Rittenhouse for resisting the urge to scream, "Too alluring for *whom*?")

"Bucky, where are you coming from? You sound like some old church lady. She's doing just what all the rest of the kids in her class are doing," said Jasmine.

"Well, your children are just not right."

Regis-Rittenhouse was losing tolerance. She restrained herself from grabbing him by the collar and mustered just enough patience to get through this speech: "So let's see if I have this right, Bucky. Your ex-wife is defective so you left her, but the children she bore are not defective. Your current wife is not defective, but the children she bore are so defective that you don't want to contaminate yours by letting them associate with hers. Buster, you've got a problem."

To his credit, Bucky seemed to be developing a sense— still formless—that she might be right. Nevertheless, tensing up and sweating through his sweat clothes, he couldn't quite reach the point of conscious vulnerability. After a brief but corpulent silence, he composed himself and demanded, "What's with marriage anyway? I just want to be happy, and I want to do it my way."

"Yeah," said Regis-Rittenhouse. And then she softened and surprised even herself, she made a rare and uncharacteristic personal disclosure: "You know, Bucky, you and I have the same problem. I can't do it my way either, so I just get out of its way. I stay single." (Love and loss were apparently on her mind. Due to her behaviors of the prior few months, we suspected that Regis-Rittenhouse had been seeing someone again—someone new—but her current wistfulness suggested that it might be over just that fast. Doppelmann remains our trusted informant on these matters.)

Regis-Rittenhouse was not at all sure how her comments went down with Bucky, but she knew she needed to break up the ice jam and relied on an old standby: Truth. "Let's get the whole family in here, all five kids. Tell them you're married and that you both have children. Then everybody can go to Bucky's apartment and have a group swim."

"Together?" asked Bucky.

"Yes, together. Make sure their measles shots are up to date and bring them all in."

They didn't come. Bucky called Regis-Rittenhouse and said that the marriage had tanked. Jasmine returned alone a few weeks later and said that Bucky was reuniting with Elise. She had told Sam and Lucy that those kids with Bucky were his own children. And when they asked why they couldn't see them again or swim in their pool, Jasmine said that Bucky didn't have a pool any more. "That's okay," said Sam. "I never wanted to swim at Bucky's place anyway. We can swim at the gym."

END OF CASE

Jasmine continues weekly visits to Regis-Rittenhouse who is educating her about the treacheries of men like Bucky and how to spot them right off. Regis-Rittenhouse is the one to do it. As for Bucky's children, they will probably miss the apartment swimming pool; however, they will have their family back, assuming that their mom will put up with their dad. Our team has only modest hope for Bucky. The man is burdened with atavistic tribal tendencies as well as an overdose of Frank Sinatra. And maybe his parents are Crustaceans who believe in their own superior endowment, although Bucky doesn't seem particularly well endowed except for those pecs and biceps. Of course, people can believe almost anything about themselves if they need to. Doppelmann, in particular, doesn't think that's all bad.

Chapter X

MARRIAGE AND THE COSMOS

The more we explored marriages and their dogging vicissitudes, the more inscrutable they became. Although they are quite corruptible, as we have pointed out, millions persist. However, they may be losing ground in this country and in a hundred years may seem just a quaint remnant of the past like whalebone corsets, dial telephones and tuna noodle casserole. The Age of Marriage, however, could last a thousand more years, which would come to a total of, say, five or ten thousand—about 145,000,000 fewer years than the Age of Dinosaurs.

If marriage does hold its own, we need to understand it better, at least as well as we understand the dinosaurs. Even though we knew that we had made some significant contributions to the marital literature up to this point—especially with our typologies of infidelity, mind reading and communication patterns, and our speciology of in-laws—we had an uneasy sense that our gifts of insight and intellectual inquiry had somehow failed us. Like spokes without an axle, our enlightening case studies and all the rest did not quite come together. We needed a centerpiece, a comprehensive theory, an explanation of how marriage actually works. Our team spent months in search of a grand unifying principle and wondered if, like logic in a squabble, it would forever elude us. Then one day:

"Well, I know what it is," said Sack.

We jerked our heads and looked at him in unison. I wondered whether in the midst of our exhaustive efforts, he had been holding out on us or is just daffy.

"Have you been holding out on us, Sack, or are you just daffy?" Regis-Rittenhouse asked.

"Nope," he said. "I already told you about Heisenberg's Uncertainty Principle … way back. Nobody was interested in the physicists."

"So you've been pouting," said Regis-Rittenhouse.

"Nope. You just weren't interested so I let it be."

"You *have* been pouting," said Regis-Rittenhouse.

"Well, now we're interested," Bloom interrupted, "and we apologize for dismissing you when we were designing our field research."

Sack sighed and began, "String theory, the theory of everything. And since marriage is part of everything, we're in. This theory says that all of the forces and particles of nature are composed of tiny vibrating strings, and it predicts that extra dimensions will be discovered. Physicists and cosmologists have to cope with a universe full of mysterious stuff that they can't see and don't understand: dark matter, dark energy, gravitational effects. And marriage counselors have to cope with the same things: dark matter, dark energy, gravitational effects. Some day all of it will come together." Sack elaborated and we listened.

Doppelmann loved it. Visions of the seen and the unseen danced in his head: black holes; antimatter; imaginary time; empty space foaming with energy; volleys of silent, invisible explosions; galaxies gliding into the farthest reaches of the universe. The more he went on about it, the clearer it became that he was envisioning the physicists as set designers for some pulsating romance, maybe Antony and Cleopatra.

"Get a grip, Doppelmann. This is science, not poetry," said Regis-Rittenhouse.

"Daniel, I'm afraid she's right," said Bloom.

Everyone but Doppelmann agreed that we must not lose ourselves in the language of the cosmos, which so bewitchingly lends itself to melodrama. We are looking at a scientific theory, a theory about the cosmos potentially *inclusive* of the baffling human relationship—not that the physicists have been rash enough to say so. Like gas molecules in a flask, millions of people randomly collide with one another. Some of them bond and emerge in pairs through some unseen force. Perhaps it's the vibrating strings. This, we hoped, would be the grand scientific design that moves us beyond our humiliating biology.

Regis-Rittenhouse expressed her doubts that the physicists have marriage and coupling in mind when they discuss string theory. Sack said, "Of course they do, but they would lose all credibility if they admitted it. Physicists are always discussing their mating issues through encryption, sometimes unconsciously. Freud would agree.

"Take Einstein," he continued. "He said that all of space is bubbling with an invisible form of energy that creates mutual repulsion between objects normally attracted to each other by gravity. Few people realize that this is code. The space he was referring to was his actual marriage; the objects, his wife and mistress and the gravity, his sexual attraction. I'll bet he wrote this stuff just as his first marriage was crashing, and the encoding would have protected his wife from knowing how he felt. Although she was brilliant, she was unstable and they had two kids, so he would have been sensitive about her feelings. Well, then Einstein went on about dark energy. I figure he was talking about his ongoing affair or maybe the alienation that he was feeling toward his wife, I don't know. Anyway, my point is that his whole life is encrypted into the language of the cosmos."

At that point, we were pressed to leave for appointments with our respective couples. I'm sure the rest of the team felt as I did, that the loft had never felt so … well, so lofty. And it was increasingly clear that Sack was surviving his depression and emerging as our most innovative thinker. He was pushing us in new directions.

Unfortunately, he had made a mistake by bringing up Einstein's personal life. Doppelmann, as you have probably gathered, becomes too easily distracted by romance, its players and the intriguing collateral damage. Sometimes when his imagination overcomes him, he doesn't let go until he has dressed the part. A few days after our discussion he showed up at work with a drooping mustache and grizzled wig. Holly fielded the comments, concerns and questions of his bewildered clientele as they left FABRCTR. Some were worried that he had aged with lightning speed, others that he was undergoing chemotherapy, but the most skeptical believed it to be a trick: an attempt to elicit more information from them than they wanted to divulge. Another receptionist might have folded under the pressure, but not Holly who had appreciated Doppelmann's gifts for masquerade from the moment they met. With the aplomb of Regis-Rittenhouse, she repeatedly said, "No, the man's just eccentric," while the rest of us, using remarkable restraint, communicated cool unconcern. He gave up the guise after a week or two.

Space and Time

We picked up on the theory of everything at our next research meeting and struggled with the thorny issue of mathematics. Physicists actually use formulas and proofs to back up their theories. With their symmetry and repetition, these are visually appealing, but about as inaccessible to us as the scratches on ancient Etruscan tablets. Proofs and formulas, of course, do not preclude the possibility that theories are incubated in the unconscious, a realm we know better than the physicists. In fact, that is probably exactly the place where they are incubated, the same place as marital turmoil and Doppelmann's fantasies. Nevertheless, mathematics is problematic for the marriage therapist who is more likely to be a scientist of the armchair variety. It has never done much for the field, or marriage for that matter, and we could not stretch our collective wits around a mathematical proof for relationships. Based on some of our previous accomplishments, however, we devised a few formulas:

$$\chi = \frac{\text{offending partner} \times \text{missing apparel}}{\text{gulled partner} + \text{espionage} + 54x} \times \frac{1}{2} \text{ assets} + \Omega$$

$$\varnothing = \text{patience} + 10^2 \times \frac{\text{slow muscle twitch}}{\text{fast muscle twitch} - \text{volley ball aptitude}^2}$$

$$\lambda = \text{audible crunching} - (\text{selective listening disorder}^2) + \sqrt{yz}$$

Perhaps in the future our equations will be more elegant and penetrating and stretch out over pages and pages. Regis-Rittenhouse suggested that in the meantime we could use some of the physicists' concepts as working models and added, "Even if we cannot back them up with *tedious* formulas."

"Be careful. We must be vigilant to avoid a creeping tendency to envy the physicists," said Bloom. "After all, eventually we will all be colleagues, collaborators with a unified vision."

We nodded in agreement, then resumed our envy of the physicists. For example, who could not envy Einstein's remarkable sleight of hand with the space-time issue? Matter and energy bend space and time, he theorized; they become warped and indistinguishable from one another. The importance of relativity theory for the marriage counselor has been underrated and very few practitioners see it as belonging on our turf, a regrettable situation. We believe that the physicists, most of them in their own relationships for good or ill, would not mind if we appropriate their terms for our discussion.

Yes. Space-time belongs to all of us, especially to married people who would do well to synchronize their space and time with one another. Once again on the cutting edge, we agreed that we would analyze the interactions of two couples—one recently sprouted, the other grown ripe—relative to space and time. Our team surmised that space-time for recently paired individuals would be less synchronized than that of a seasoned couple, that the edges would be jagged and rough like the Tetons. To explore this, Bloom carefully examined the experiences of one of her couples.

Ted and Elise

Ted and Elise, both in their twenties, had been married just a year or two when they came to FABRCTR. They tripped over their differences as frequently as they were tripping over one another's magazines on the floor. Bloom focused on one of their differences and asked that they recount their conversation as precisely as they could. Ted had begun with an innocent question:

"Have we seen *Mulholland Drive*?"

"We saw *Mulholland Drive* with my brother, remember?"

"No, that was *Memento*. Then we went to Pop's Pizza and Josh complained about it for an hour, all the way through beer and dinner."

"No, he was complaining about *Mulholland Drive*. And only for a few minutes. He had already seen *Memento* and, remember, he was so impressed with the main guy because he was using his own body as a PalmPilot. He told us he was going out the next day to get some tattoos, phone numbers, birthdays, stuff like that."

"He had his tattoos months before he saw *Memento*."

"He didn't have them at the family reunion."

"Yes, he did. Your Aunt Louise was gossiping about it, tsk-tsking. Remember?"

"My brother did not have tattoos at the family reunion, and Aunt Louise was tsk-tsking about his nose ring, your shirt and my sister's tank top."

During our team discussion Regis-Rittenhouse became impatient with the muddle, so she shook it out and organized the following space-time lines:

Elise's Space-Time Line	Ted's Space-Time Line
	Josh gets tattoos.
Family reunion: Aunt Louise disapproves of Josh's nose ring, Ted's shirt and Elise's sister's tank top.	Elise's family reunion: Her Aunt Louise disapproves of Josh's tattoos.
Josh sees *Memento.*	Elise, Ted and Josh see *Memento.*
Josh gets tattoos.	Dinner with Josh; he complains about the movie for an hour and a half.
Elise, Ted and Josh see *Mulholland Drive.*	Ted puzzles about whether he has ever seen the movie *Mulholland Drive.*
Dinner with Josh; he complains about the movie for a few minutes.	Elise is all messed up on her time frame.
Ted forgets that they have seen *Mulholland Drive.*	

Bloom suggested to Elise and Ted that they call Josh to straighten this out, but they procrastinated until it became a dead issue—as she suspected they would. (Avoidance is a fine strategy for those risk-averse to exposure of error.) After obtaining permission to talk to Josh, she called him herself, "All in the name of research." She identified herself and inquired about the family reunion. Josh said, "Ah, no, I didn't do the reunion thing this year. Aunt Louise, I can't take her, and Elise is getting just as bad. Man, what's with my sister, Shrink Lady? Ever since she got married ... Anyway, me and my band drove to Fargo that weekend for a gig. Had to miss it. How'd it go?" Bloom said that she had not had the pleasure of attending and asked him about his tattoos.

"Nah, I'm not messing with that stuff anymore. One time when I was high—three, maybe four years ago—I was just a kid—I paid this dude to tattoo an eagle on my back, spread clear from one armpit to the other. I'm just glad I don't have to see it. And my girlfriend at the time, Nicki ... I have her name on my arm, and we broke up three years ago, so now I'm walking around with this Nicki thing inside a heart on my biceps and she means nothing to me, man. That wasn't smart. Then I saw this movie, *Memory,* I think it was."

"*Memento?*"

"Yeah, that was it. Did you see it too? Bizarre, all in reverse. Time went backwards and this guy couldn't remember anything, so he tattooed stuff all over his body so he'd have it. Right after the movie, I thought, wouldn't that be sweet? I could just lift up my pant leg and those digits would be right there. But, no, man, then I remembered how I screwed myself over with that stuff already, and everybody's phone numbers are always changing, cell phones and all. No more tattoos."

"Who did you see the movie with?"

"I dunno, man. Friends, definitely not Nicki, some dude … probably Hank. What's with the scrutiny?"

'I'm doing some research on space and time in relationships."

"Cool. Call any time, Shrink Lady."

Our team skipped an analysis of Josh's space-time line. The *Memento*-Pop's Pizza-family reunion saga had developed a labyrinthine quality. The point had been made: Josh was unequivocally in a different space and different time than either Ted or Elise, but more importantly, Ted and Elise, still married neophytes, would need quite a few years to synchronize their space-time capsules. Bloom is not at all sure that their patience will hold out.

END OF CASE

After exploring the space-time dimension in a marriage of neophytes, our team was ready to explore that dimension with the most enduring couple we know, Harold and Ev, whom you may remember from the mind reading chapter. They're the ones who still don't live in Florida. This time I interviewed them because Bloom was exhausted after all the ramifications of the Ted and Elise case.

Harold and Ev Redux

I started with Harold alone and just let the man ramble while I decided where to burrow in. Back when the children were young and there was no cabin in Wisconsin, the household was pretty frantic, he told me, and the summers darn hard.

He'd been a bricklayer before he started his own construction company and worked overtime to keep up with the bills. When he got home, he played ball with the kids if it was still light outside. Within moments of helping them get to bed, he was snoozing himself. "But," he said, "that wasn't enough for me. I'm the kinda guy who needs a little time to himself. Hell, Doc, I'm a fisherman. So on weekends I'd get up before everybody else, brew some coffee and head down the road to a little lake for some crappie fishin'. Wasn't much more 'un a pond and still as a dead man ... sun comin' up, and I sat on the edge of a big rock—I named it Rocky. Had my fishin' line and my thermos of coffee. Nothin' like it in the whole world.

"Then Ev—God bless her—she got it in her head that Hal Junior, our first, should go fishin' with me. He was seven, maybe eight. And, ya know, I love that kid, but fishin' with him just wasn't the same. I had to get him up, poor sleepy kid ... never ready, but I did it for awhile. Then Ev said, 'Take Katy too.' She was maybe five. Well, I knew Ev had her hands full—Susie just a baby and Richie no more 'un three—but that was the only time I ever got to myself. After a few times takin' 'em both, I must of come off pretty forlorn without even knowin' it 'cause Ev started askin' me a lot of questions and then said I should get medical help. 'Hell, woman,' I said, 'I don't need medical help.' Well, she said I sure needed somethin'. And I thought about it and scratched my chin and stared at her and stared at my fishin' pole over in the corner of the kitchen and at the thermos, saw Rocky and the sun comin' up over that lake in my mind's eye and it all fit into those Saturday mornings like crappies in a pail. So I said to her, 'I need my fishin' time to myself.' And Ev, she knew it. She's a damn good woman."

Harold considers himself a simple man with simple pleasures, and this idea seemed simple enough to him: Every time
he went down to that lake, the world was being created again
for the first time. Nothing came before, nothing after. When
he was on that rock with his pole, he was in never-changing
space-time that circled round him, wrapped him up.

Then I talked to Ev who corroborated Harold's story. "Yes,"
she said, "he needed his fishing time." Meanwhile she had
been home with the four children. Although she encouraged
them to sleep in on weekends—well, maybe until 7:00—this
encouragement was entirely lost on the younger ones. No
space and time bended and blended for her out on that rock;
instead the house became an eternal space where the children
would never grow old. Surely Richie's grip on that stuffed bear
and his erratic toilet habits were forever suspended in space
and time. In her always-present future she saw herself accom-
panying him to middle school where she would hold Teddy
while Richie did his business in the boy's room. And there
were the homemade birthday cards which all appeared to be
recycled. Every year the same silly bunny with the same goofy
smile and the same scrawl materialized as sure as the March
melt.

We wondered if any of the other players would corrob-
orate the Harold and Ev story. So with their permission, we
interviewed their oldest son Hal Junior, now 62, and Gladys,
a neighbor when their children were young. Hal said he had
never gone fishing with his dad on those Saturdays. "No, that
was Dad's time, and we all knew it. Besides I would've had
to get out of bed. Never would've done it; the man left before
dawn. But I can remember him and Mom arguing about it. I

think she had some Norman Rockwell notion that Dad and I should fish together. Maybe Katy went with him once or twice."

Then I checked with Gladys by telephone. She is 83 and living in Florida. "I saw that man headed back home with his pail of crappies every Saturday during fishing season and even when it wasn't fishing season, and he refused to take his children. Can you imagine? Ev would come over and cry on my shoulder, poor woman, those four rambunctious kids ... crazy, and he's off playing fisherman with himself. Crappies, they're hardly edible. And to top it all off, he refused to move to Florida." Gladys actually had more to say, but I thanked her for her participation in our research and said goodbye.

END OF CASE

Although Harold and Ev were each in their own space-time capsules, there seems to have been no serious extraterrestrial collision, though maybe a few scrapes. Although very poor at mind reading, as you may remember, they seem to have some sixth sense about navigating around one another's space-time. Well, maybe just Ev has a sixth sense. Harold has the fishing pole, the quiet lakeside, the rising sun and the thermos of coffee, which all fold into one another, into the space and into the early morning as seamlessly as the memories of two dozen childhood beach excursions become one, a single experience that recurs spontaneously with a whiff of sea air or a graze of sand. Whatever anyone else around them does, those two seem to bend space and time in their own inimitable synchronization.

Any individual who is mated in any way would do well to bone up on the space-time warp in his own life. What we see as reality is just a creation of the mind. With memories of what happened when and where, partners fold space into time, past into present and fantasy into reality the way a dessert chef folds fluffy beaten egg whites into flour and sugar. Experiences become configured and reconfigured: the year we lived by the railroad track, the summer Scooter broke his leg, the day you totaled the car, love-making during the blizzard, love-making while the baby was sleeping, love-making while we skipped classes (different guy, sorry), our first kiss, our last kiss. This abundance can result in harmony, bitterness or boredom. In stable marriages partners seem willing to co-mingle their experiences and come to some kind of subliminal agreement about their respective pasts or simply to live with the disjunction. This may be the key to the longevity of their relationship.

A New Frontier of Marital Research

The niggling question that lay before us was this: How could we use our space-time insights to help our couples? They often need something, well, more concrete. Once again, the FABRCTR team was not at a loss. To clarify the point for our couples, we created the concept of the Space-Time Pouch, well, actually Doppelmann did. He had a new leather satchel and many versions of its rich significance. Anyway, our team defined the Space-Time Pouch as an imaginary pocket for experiences (see Glossary). Think contents of a woman's purse. A single woman may have a tampon, possibly a condom, keys for her own place, another set for her boyfriend's place, a cell phone, an extra pair of panty hose, concert tickets and dental floss. A young mother may have an extra diaper, a bundle of Kleenex, a pacifier, a copy of *Runaway Bunny,* animal crackers and dental floss. An older woman ... well, you get the gist. These contents are like the persons's experiences in Space-Time Pouches, shifting from day to day and differing from one person to the next. Precise time and space often seem indispensable in our everyday lives, but no one expects the contents of a woman's purse to be stable, predictable or precise. Our team hopes that this will help couples to accept that there is no absolute couple past, present or future. Each partner must allow the other his or her own experience. Tattoos before, after the family reunion, bodies present or absent in that space, just live with it. Although this uncertainty may make some of you uneasy, consider the advantage: You will be more amiable and accommodating instead of degenerating into a huff and arrogantly insisting on the superiority and accuracy of your own pouch contents.

Sack became so energized by our ongoing discussion of space and time that his depression was lifting and his smoking breaks disappearing. Then one day he announced that he would be gone for a few days because he was driving down to Fermilab to check out the physicists. By concocting a story about an article he was writing for a psychological journal on the role of dark matter in the lives of the depressed, he acquired a press pass. He took a tour, saw the particle accelerator, chatted at some length with an Argentine physicist named Jorgelina and reported back to us. Among other things, she told him that physicists believe that 90% of the universe is composed of dark matter. She was certainly telling the right person; Sack had had his suspicions.

He made a second, then a third trip. The more information he brought back to us, the more convinced we became that the physical world of the universe mirrors the emotional world of the married. For example, subatomic events occur in a cloud of uncertainty and that is exactly where relationship events occur. And physicists talk about a vacuum of space that they say is not vacuous at all. This describes our couples who complain of empty marriages that are not empty, but are stuffed with resentment, regrets and secrets—virtual atomic buzz. And what about the displacement of an electron? The "hole" that it leaves behind, which may or may not be a hole, behaves like a positively charged particle. When Sack described this to us, he was not even aware that he was describing his own life. Shirley's departure left a void and here he was, all charged up.

Among the most promising material that Sack presented from Fermilab were the bubble chamber photographs which show sequences of particle collisions and decays. Our team deemed these to have particular relevance to marital issues. Doppelmann agreed to study them, which he did. "Ah, these are like Calder mobiles delicately transfigured into two dimensions," he reported back to us. We were not sure what the physicists would say about this, but then we did not have to tell them about Doppelmann. Besides, none of us know any physicists except for the occasional one who comes in with his partner and is too wrapped up in his marital conundrums to be of any use, and then, of course, Sack now knows Jorgelina.

The case of Elise, Ted and Josh presented a fine opportunity to simulate the particle photographs. Doppelmann said he could envision them already. Bloom was apprehensive because we seemed to be lapsing into metaphor again, but we just couldn't help ourselves. (Besides, metaphor and pure science may not be so far apart after all.) Figure 1 demonstrates how Doppelmann depicted the couple's movie-tatoo interplay.

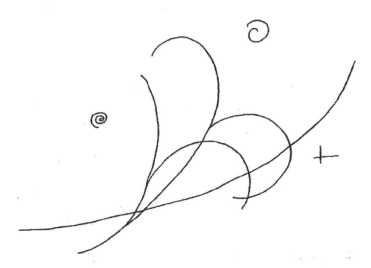

Figure 1. Bubble Chamber: This figure is a simulation of the unfolding of the divergent experiences of Elise and Ted. Josh's further divergence swept through the field without heed for what had already been established.

We were quite pleased with these results and were ready to go ahead with more complex interactions. Elise and Ted gave us their consent to interview the other family members. They were all very cooperative, except for Elise's grandfather who had little truck with "*pro*-fessionals who mess with people's heads." We got a good read on him just the same.

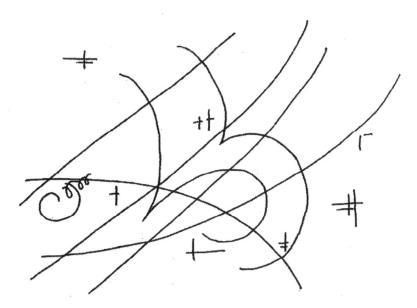

Figure 2. Bubble Chamber: This simulation represents the divergent experiences of Elise, Ted and Josh when the field is opened up to the experiences of other family members present or not present at the family reunion. (Grandfather is in the upper left-hand corner.)

We asked Sack to take our simulations to Jorgelina the next time he visited Fermilab. He did, and apparently she complimented FABRCTR on its creative and unorthodox enterprise, but implied that the simulations could not really be categorized as science. "They may hold some promise for future research," she said.

Some envy of the physicists remains intact. We want to be able to do what they do, that is, to observe the natural world, explain it and make accurate predictions. But even the physicists struggle. Although they can make predictions about the whole cosmos, they often fail to do the same with a few infinitesimal particles, which may not be particles at all, but waves. At least we know that people are people, but, of course, we can predict very little about them. Well, sure, that millions will watch the Super Bowl and hardly anyone will watch public-access TV, but we cannot predict the outcome of individual heart-wrenching relationships accurately or consistently. The physicists may know that the mass of the universe is dark matter, but they don't know exactly what dark matter is. They are not like the food people who can say with assurance that the pretzels in this bag are composed of soft red wheat flour, corn syrup, salt, vegetable oil, sodium bicarbonate and yeast. We are not like the food people either because we do not know what composes personal dark matter, so maybe it's a draw.

In the end we decided to leave string theory to the physicists who will someday make sense of it. We do not feel like failures. After all, we have been visionaries and travelers, and if marriage lasts, it may some day become part of the grand theory of everything. It was enough for Christopher Columbus—Leif Erickson, the Chinese or whomever—just to discover America. No one expected them to set up its infrastructure.

The Wrap

A RATHER CURIOUS SORT OF LIFE

Since putting marriage in the context of the cosmos, we have gained respect for it. The concept of two persons partnering for life has assumed a sort of nobility, even though its reality often demoralizes the best-intentioned people. No glide through Disney World, it's more like a carriage ride through a rutted street. Marriage itself is a problem, it's true, but so are the players and their circumstances. Egos collide like bumper cars, household chores annoy like radio static, and normality withers like a utopian ideal.

"Lord, what fools these mortals be!" Doppelmann, with his literary take. We had gathered in the loft for the grand wrap-up of our long exploration and were concluding that humans are limited in their marital aptitude. And the bungling of the mortal seems to begin with the bungling of the choice. Regis-Rittenhouse has long contended that young women run headlong into a calamitous conjugal situation because of their vaulted ambitions to have a wedding. She faults gown makers, florists and *Modern Bride* for perpetuating the folly. If she is correct about this, a woman—perhaps of any age—is in no condition to make a wise choice.

But there are other dubious reasons for marriage. For centuries both men and women seem to have been motivated to marry to secure a sexual partner, although this has ceased to be an issue in this country for all but the most restrained individuals. Still others believe that marriage is good for their health like oatmeal, apples and amino acids and, of course, others marry simply to have children. "Or maybe because they are already having children," said Bloom. "That's how we got started." Synchronized head jerks again. Bloom blushed and said it is on her mind now because her oldest daughter is a 17-year old (a *lush* 17-year old, I might add).

Doppelmann and Sack believe the match is all, that the fate of the marriage rests on an auspicious pairing. Concerning the matter of inauspicious pairing, however, Bloom raised a troubling concern within our own church walls. Eddie, whom the reader may remember as our first receptionist, wandered back into the church, discovered Holly and now materializes regularly for a chat with her. Bloom is distressed to observe that Holly, generally a sensible young woman who has developed artful tactics for purging telemarketers as well as unwanted wayfarers, is bending to Eddie's charms. Except for Doppelmann, the group agreed that this match is not an auspicious pairing.

Then he reminded us of the Glen and Birdie episode, fondly noted by the team as his El Greco faux pas. As inauspicious as their first interview with him may have been, the couple was actually a quick study and resolved their contention expeditiously. He submits that if each partner has selected the other with the deep natural clairvoyance Glen and Birdie apparently had, the couple can endure not only an ill-favored visage, but complaints, ruin, upheaval and sorrow. He held forth for several minutes until Regis-Rittenhouse excused herself to find the lectern. Sack went after her and told her it was long gone. "Besides," he said, "it wouldn't be worth the time and effort just for a little sarcasm about Doppelmann's oratory." The rest of us agreed with her suggestion, however, that the concept of clairvoyance is too eccentric for serious researchers like ourselves and that the physicists would unlikely have even a particle of respect for it.

We continued our discussion of the match with a general consensus that a couple who may be a good fit at one point in life may not be a good fit later on. Timing then is the critical thing. It is hazardous to marry too early or too late, but it may be most hazardous to marry at just the right time because this tends to give the partners unwarranted confidence, which reduces vigilance. Then, of course, some people with no diagnosable deficiency whatsoever are simply unsuitable for marriage at any time. This could include as much as 20% of the population, maybe more. "They should just not marry," said Bloom, "but who will tell them?"

Before we could tell them, we would have to figure out who they are. When we scanned our case studies, the only ones we unanimously agreed would fall into this category are Lang, Architect of Postmodern Botch, whose keen memory trapped all of his wife's mistakes, and Biceps Bucky, Architect of Having-it-My-Way. Clearly it had been too late to tell them when they came to FABRCTR, and they wouldn't have listened anyway. What Lang and Bucky need is social engineering, but we're marriage counselors, not social engineers. Lang, Bucky, the natterers and the dispensers of faint praise, all of them could use it, a chip in the brain, something.

Regis-Rittenhouse said there were women who shouldn't marry as well. "Like me," she said, "and young women who bring disgrace upon themselves when they marry just to have a wedding." While the latter is an astute observation, it was one she had already made and she wouldn't let go of it, not even after we all agreed about the perils of bride fever. I wondered what was in her craw and on a hunch asked her what was happening on the dating scene. "I'm done with the last one," she said. "And besides, I don't like his surname: Smits."

"What?"

"His last name is Smits."

"What does that have to do with it?"

"I married a Rittenhouse, then I married a Regis, and I kept their names because they suit me. Smits doesn't suit me."

Dopplemann agreed; the name Smits would never do. He was apparently overlooking the news that she had been married and not once, but twice. However, that seemed to be enough revelation for now, so we let the matter drop after noting that some people might be motivated to marry just for a name.

"Whatever people marry for, once in, they're free to mess it up," said Sack. "And sometimes it only takes one of them." Although this was unmitigated and poorly disguised Shirley carping, he isn't thinking much about her lately. Most weekends he travels to Chicago where he meets Jorgelina, and occasionally she comes to town. On these occasions poor Hobbes plays second fiddle and spends the night back on his cushion in the kitchen corner.

The group agreed that not only is marriage inherently flawed, but that humans make bad choices and often follow them up with bad behavior, or good choices and follow them up with bad behavior. Regardless of choice or behavior, however, random and otherwise unheralded events occur and can change everything. These events can be natural or man-made,[15] global, local or personal, and their impact on a marriage is widely variable. Natural disasters, even imaginary ones like Sally's Flood of '92, can have a salutary effect on a marriage. Earthquakes, droughts and war that do not kill the parties involved can actually bring them together. Communities unite against a common enemy and so can couples.

Doppelmann said that he and Nedra became resolutely united following a fateful and harrowing event with a common enemy. Early in their marriage she had practiced as a past-life regression specialist in the basement of an aging office building.[16] One evening when Doppelmann came to pick her up, she didn't show. When he went to her office door, it was locked. He knocked. No one answered. Then he heard a suspicious rustling and possibly a footstep or two. Mischief was afoot and he was the one to deal with it. He went back outside, leapt into the window well, stealthily loosened the screen, jiggled the sash, slithered inside and crept into Nedra's office where he found her tied up in beaded rope and shivering from fright in a corner. A large man wielding a closed umbrella that he apparently

---

[15]One could argue that man-made disasters are merely a subset of natural disasters in that man is part of nature, but we are near the end and do not wish to trouble the reader with further niggling.

[16]Note that I wasn't so far off when I envisioned her as a psychic. See Introduction.

believed was a rapier loomed over her. Doppelmann wrested the umbrella from him and thrust its tip to his heart. The man dropped to the floor, then moaned in the agony of death. Doppelmann freed Nedra who pulled herself together, then explained to Doppelmann that in one of this man's past lives he had been a Samurai warrior who died by sword in battle. Now, unwounded, he lay on her floor. Although he was quite harmless because he believed that he was dead, and hence his soul was busy transmigrating into its next life, Doppelmann called the police who promptly came and hauled the man away while one of them mumbled, "It takes all kinds."

That was Nedra's last customer because the two of them agreed that the past-life business is too risky. She has apparently worshiped Doppelmann as her hero ever since—at least he says so, and he has cherished his rescued maiden. This random event burnishes their marital roles, probably for life.

But random and unforeseen events, even events that seem fortuitous, can also pull couples apart. Before Jake, I was briefly married to a professional hockey player. Nearly overnight he became a celebrity, a plight which single-handedly encouraged random women to parade through his life. I left the parade and the marriage with dispatch. (I was not willing to send *him* to the garage with his *collection* of women.) Bloom repeated that sometimes a marital affair, if it doesn't destroy a marriage, can unsettle it enough to improve it. Well, that was not my experience with the Big Puck, but still she's right, it happens.

So it is, if your unfortunate selection of a mate doesn't defeat your marriage, a tornado, open manhole or job promotion may do. But even if you believe that things are going well, the black vultures will have more luck with it than you do. To this Regis-Rittenhouse says, "Nonsense, what do they have to do with it? Black vultures all look alike. What does it matter?" Bloom cautioned her to be careful because her comment has the ring of political incorrectness and speculated that black vultures probably don't all look alike to one another.[17]

Although we know that throughout our exploration into the crevices of marriage, we have enlightened ourselves and perhaps the reader as well, something about marriage still seems out of reach "Like the drawings of stags and bulls in the caves of Lascaux," said Doppelmann.

"It's the mystery," said Sack.

Yes, no matter how closely we look at marriage, something odd and mysterious remains. Consider again Hank and Traci of the slipshod shoe and laundry scene. Like many couples, they may actually prefer marriage over single, free-range living, and this in spite of serious doubts about a partner's sanity, qualms about his odor or headaches from the cacophony of messy, insatiable children. Dance careers are subverted, great books unwritten and heroic adventures sacrificed. Marriage is its own adventure.

"I almost wish I hadn't gone down the rabbit hole—and yet—and yet—it's rather curious, you know, this sort of life." Doppelmann again, with his literary take.

---

[17]Reader commentary is invited at FABRCTR5@gmail.com.

Glossary

Alice: A gifted child whose odyssey rivaled that of Odysseus himself.

Audible Crunching: An example of redundancy.

Autobiographical Memory: The part of your memory that is made up of facts and situations about your life, keeps you abreast of who you are and without which some partnerships would run more smoothly.

Bargaining: Useful for getting your way and a deal on a T-shirt in Puerta Vallarta.

BigWhopper Pick-up Truck: Often red or black, this vehicle serves as protection against the possibility that its driver may be perceived as low on testosterone.

Binturong: Arboreal animal native to the sub-tropics and not recommended for domestic living in Northern climates.

Bladder Control: A skill which inspires rivalry within a marriage.

Bloviation: Puffed-up talking.

Cherry Bomb: Type of infidelity which comes to light and causes an explosion, or less commonly, if the Gulled Partner is a particularly unexpressive type, an implosion.

Comzac: Popular drug abundantly prescribed in the eighties and nineties.

Counter-interference: Problem that arises in marital therapy when a couple unwittingly agitates the thought processes of their therapist.

Counter-quirk: Behavior either intrinsically present or developed over the course of a relationship that fits neatly, for good or ill, with the quirk of a partner. Think tongue in groove. After a couple has been together for a time, it becomes impossible to differentiate between a quirk and a counter-quirk. (See also Quirk)

Coyness: Behavior in women no longer considered chic (in some circles).

Crestfallen: Individual who is deeply disappointed that his partner is an incompetent mind reader.

Cumbersome Conscience: Type of infidelity which causes excessive guilt in the Offending Partner.

Dissembling: Among Nature's more clever and utilized inventions.

Docile Recalcitrant: Obedient, conforming and often cheerful individual who does the right things, but stubbornly adheres to getting it all wrong.

Domestic Denial: Tendency for one partner, especially the male, to believe that he actually does his fair share of the necessary household tasks.

Eye Rolling: Controversial mode of communicating.

Far Cries: A type of couple who attempts to communicate with one another from great distances without the aid of technology, clairvoyance or handwriting.

Faint Praise: Weak disguise for an insult.

Free-ranging human: A person over 18 years of age who is not married or otherwise partnered.

Gossip: An entertaining form of human communication. (It is not clear whether other species have a knack for it.)

Gulled Partner (GP): Partner to whom it is done.

Half-life: The time required for half of your memory to fail.

Half-Wit: A partner who believes that half of his memory has not yet failed.

Haroldese: The communication style of your male partner.

Heisenberg Principle: You'll always be getting in the way. No matter what.

Hormones: Tricksters that fool you into wanting sex.

Hero: A mythical character.

Inaudible Crunching: An imaginary activity.

Incidentally Acquired Kin: Kin begotten as a byproduct of marriage, most commonly in-laws and stepchildren. You may share a common ancestor with these persons, but if so, said ancestor precedes the Age of Dinosaurs.

Incontinent Psyche: Mind with a switch that is easily tripped.

Lecturee: The one who has to listen to it.

Little Remarks: Spoken grievances about in-laws, poorly disguised as mere observation.

Logical Consequences: What happens when you leave something alone, like a piece of driftwood that eventually bobs its way to shore or a malfunctioning toaster that eventually electrocutes its owner.

Love: A score of zero in tennis.

Maiden: A singular sort of female believed to have existed during the Middle Ages, although some scholars have insisted that a few were actually identified during the nineteenth century.

Marriage: Union commonly composed of two people, and if so, one from each gender, but not always; who probably live together and who plan to be together in the future, at least for the time being.

Memory-by-Proxy: Imaginary or trivial material that fills the spaces in the brain vacated by actual facts, events, feelings and ideas.

Mind Reading: A futile, nevertheless very popular activity among married people who apparently use it as a handy substitute for the entangled task of fact finding.

Mutual Repulsion Between Objects: Speculated by Sack to be Einstein's description of his own collapsing marriage.

Nap: A celestial experience, and if it's your experience, unlikely to be appreciated by your partner.

Nattering: A diarrhetic form of talking.

Offending Partner (OP): Partner who does it.

Pin-Striping: Popular way to gain female attention in the 1950s.

Postmodern Botch: The fantasy, complexity or ornamentation generated by an obsessive concern with the mistakes and flaws of another person.

Quirk: A behavior infinitely resistant to extinction that appears unreasonable to everyone but the person behaving. (See also Counter-Quirk)

Relieved Type: Individual who is deeply grateful that her partner is an incompetent mind reader.

Romance: Brief love affair.

Sanguine-Confident Type: Individual who is absolutely convinced that she can read the mind of her partner and refuses to acknowledge error even when proved wrong.

Sanguine-Indifferent Type: Individual who claims that he has never engaged in mind reading and never gives it a thought.

Selective Listening Disorder: Common malady unfairly believed to be up to the discretion of the disordered individual.

Shrug: Type of infidelity that rarely causes alarm because the Gulled Partner is kept in the dark and the Offending Partner's conscience stays in check.

Space-Time Pouch: Imaginary pocket for your experiences of space and time; a place where they blend together in unpredictable and infinitely unique ways, like the contents of a woman's purse.

Specious Reasoning: The reasoning that makes it possible for you to marry someone even after you have met the family.

Two-Peas-in-a-Pod Stage: Commonly observed early stage of a relationship in which a couple believes that they agree on all things great and small.

Vigilant-Agitated Type: Individual always grazing for information about how his partner will fulfill his fantasies, expectations and desires. Typically, he uses this information to calculate the most auspicious moment in which to make an amorous move.

Vigilant-Shuttered Type: Individual fearful that his partner may actually have some mind reading skills and adjusts his behavior accordingly,

Sovereignty: Dominion over one's own person in time and space, especially with regard to eating, drinking and naps.

Watipi: Elk.

Werner Karl Heisenberg: A physicist.

About the Author and the Manuscript

Jean K. Wolf, PhD, Licensed Psychologist, had a private psychotherapy practice in St. Paul, Minnesota, from 1980 until she retired in 2010. She loved people: friends, neighbors, anyone she happened to meet. Engaging her intellect, personality and intuition to help people in their relationships was immensely satisfying for her.

Jean wrote this manuscript in her spare time during 2000–2003. It was her chance to indulge her love of language in a playful way and to give free rein to her lively wit. When the manuscript was complete, she gave herself a deadline for finding a publisher. The deadline arrived; she put her manuscript in her file cabinet. In 2004 Jean was appointed to the Minnesota State Board of Psychology where she served until 2012. The manuscript stayed in her file cabinet.

Jean died in February 2020. Her book is published as a loving tribute to a life lived with purpose and gentle good humor.

John Wolf
(Jean's husband for fifty-five years.
In case you wonder, I was never banished to the garage.)
Minneapolis, Minnesota, June 2020

Made in the USA
Monee, IL
19 September 2020